a SAVOR THE SOUTH® *cookbook*

Okra

VIRGINIA WILLIS

The University of North Carolina Press CHAPEL HILL

The paper in this book meets the guidelines for permanence and durability of
the Committee on Production Guidelines for Book Longevity of the Council on
Library Resources. The University of North Carolina Press has been a member
of the Green Press Initiative since 2003.

Library of Congress Cataloging-in-Publication Data
Willis, Virginia, 1966–
Okra : a savor the South cookbook / Virginia Willis.
pages cm. — (Savor the South cookbooks)
Includes bibliographical references and index.
ISBN 978-1-4696-1442-7 (cloth : alk. paper)
1. Cooking (Okra) 2. Cooking, American — Southern style.
3. International cooking. 4. Okra. I. Title.
TX803.O37.W55 2014
641.6′5648 — dc23   2013033254

18 17 16 15 14   5 4 3 2 1

To my sweet mama, Jenny B. Willis,
who taught me to love food and cooking

Contents

Global Okra Recipes 55

AFRICA

NORTH AFRICA AND THE MEDITERRANEAN

a SAVOR THE SOUTH® *cookbook*

Okra

Introduction

ODE TO OKRA

Okra is a contentious vegetable. It's one of the most southern of vegetables and as much a part of southern cuisine as collard greens and field peas, but it's far more controversial in the southern kitchen than those comforting, homey sides. Folks love okra or they hate it. No one—veritably no one—is in the middle.

Okra lovers passionately love okra in all manners of being, all shapes, forms, and means of preparation. Boiled, fried, steamed, grilled, broiled, pickled, raw, whole, sliced, julienned—you name it, okra lovers love okra. Those who hate it think it's slimy, gooey, and gummy. In my opinion, they just haven't met the right okra.

As a southern food writer, I embrace my membership in the former camp. I love okra. I enjoy it cooked in a myriad of ways and combinations. And I love a challenge. I will cajole, entice, and seduce doubters into becoming believers. I rejoice in converting people to the joys of cooking, eating, and savoring okra. I'm an okra missionary.

Okra's Southern Connections

The recent upsurge in the popularity of southern cooking across the United States has brought renewed attention to okra. Chefs and home cooks across the country are exploring okra dishes far beyond gumbo. Heirloom okra seed packets are finding their way into the hands of gardeners all over the South. The long, slender, fingerlike pods of Red Burgundy; multicolored Hill Country Red okra, which is perfect for pickling; and short stubby pods of Star of David are joining the popular Clemson Spineless in the southern garden.

Okra thrives in the South. It loves the heat. The plant soars majestically as tall as ten feet high and produces large leaves and luxurious flowers that resemble hibiscus. Indeed, okra is a member of the mallow family, along with hibiscus, hollyhocks, and cotton, other familiar plants in our subtropical region.

Paper-thin, butter-yellow, wrinkled petals whirl together and are each punctuated with a brilliant dot of burgundy near the okra flower's center. Out of this shoots an erect stamen dusted with vibrant yellow pollen. Once unfurled, the petals wilt in the afternoon and usually fall to the ground the following day. The plant is sensual poetry.

Okra not only has an enticing flower, but it's a seductive vegetable as well. No other vegetable in the southern garden shares its particular colors. Within the pods is a generosity of seeds, nestled in orderly fashion in chambers. The slender, curving fingers are covered with the palest, most delicate down. The plant is lush, fecund, and sultry yet hearty, robust, and sturdy. Okra is overtly feminine and masculine all at once. The plant seems to embrace adversity, tolerating poor soil as well as being among the most heat- and drought-tolerant vegetables. Okra willfully extorts the heat of a scorching southern summer like a Tennessee Williams character, making it a perfect match for the Deep South.

Culinary Uses

Okra can be prepared in a vast number of ways. I enjoy it stewed and so slick it barely needs chewing. Crisply fried, grilled with charred bits, roasted and chewy, or in a soup or stew, I love okra. I like to think of it as the next asparagus. It's only a matter of time before the love of okra spreads. I'm convinced.

Okra is perhaps most famous as a common ingredient in the classic Louisiana dish, gumbo. (Okra helps thicken Creole gumbo; the other choice for thickening gumbo is filé, or sassafras powder.) It has a long history in Louisiana, where it was popular with the French colonists and thrives in the moist heat. Much of my childhood was spent in Louisiana—perhaps that's where my love for okra took root. Or perhaps it was in my grandmother's kitchen, eating crispy, cornmeal-crusted fried okra.

Fried okra is a southern staple. When I was working in France for cookbook author Anne Willan, we once needed okra to test a recipe. It was nowhere to be found in the local markets, so we had to order a case from the French wholesale market Rungis, on the outskirts of Paris, only to use less than a pound! The gumbo was a huge disappointment, falling short of Anne's strict standards. With the rest of the case, I made fried okra, using the only ground corn available in France at the time, fine polenta, for the coating. Anne called it "popcorn-fried okra," and it was a huge hit. I can pretty much guarantee that this was the only time in history that fried okra was enjoyed as a snack with apéritifs before dinner anywhere, much less in France. Another classic combination is okra and tomatoes. It's a natural marriage; the flavors, textures, and growing seasons are made for each other. In fact, these two classic southern treatments are found in almost every country that has okra in its cuisine, India, Greece, and Egypt included. Both combinations clearly work.

Historical References

Little is known about the early history and botanical distribution of okra, but it's thought to have originated near the equator in Africa, in the area that includes present-day Ethiopia and the eastern portion of the Anglo-Egyptian Sudan. It eventually made its way into northern Africa, the Mediterranean, and India before its journey across the Atlantic to the New World. According to *The New Encyclopedia of Southern Culture*, enslaved Africans brought okra to the Americas during the era of the West African slave trade.

There are two primary theories on the etymology of the word "gumbo." The first suggests that in Bantu, the language family of southern Africa, which includes Swahili, okra is called *ngumbo*, and this is where "gumbo" originated. The second is that "gumbo" comes from the Portuguese corruption, *quingombo*, for the word *quillobo*, the native name for the okra plant in the Congo and Angola.

Okra is found, however, in regions well beyond Africa and the American South. The ancient routes by which okra was taken from Central Africa to Egypt to the eastern Mediterranean and to India are not certain, but we do know that okra is found in abundance not only in the United States, but also in East Africa, India, and Southeast Asia. It's also found in pockets in the Caribbean, as well as in South America. One thing is for certain—if the weather is hot, okra will grow.

Botanical Features

Because I want this book to be a one-stop shop for okra, I have included information about how to cultivate and grow the plant below. Let's dig in the dirt and find out more about our hot-headed, exotic edible.

ROOTS

Towering okra plants require a sturdy base. The root system consists of two parts: a shallow, spreading system that branches out to a distance of 6 feet on all sides of the plant and a deeply penetrating, well-branched taproot up to 2 inches thick and 4½ feet deep.

STEM

The pale green okra stem is semi-woody and often tinged with darker green or red. It's straight and erect with many short branches that are spaced approximately 4–6 inches apart.

LEAVES

The okra leaf is dark green and somewhat resembles a fig leaf. The heart-shaped leaves are approximately 6–8 inches across and up to 12 inches in length. They're covered in a hairy, fuzzy down that, in contact with bare skin, produces redness and irritation. Harvesting okra can be somewhat challenging—in fact, the expression "it will eat you up" comes to mind. It's advisable to wear long sleeves even in the hottest summer months when picking okra to prevent inflammation and itching.

FLOWERS

Okra flowers are large, around 2 inches in diameter, with five white to yellow petals with a red or purple dot at the base of each petal. The flower lasts for only one day, then falls away. Each blossom develops a small green nub that becomes the okra fruit.

FRUIT

Okra is cultivated for its fibrous fruits, known as pods, which contain an abundance of round seeds. The edible, tapered pods are harvested while still tender and immature. The pod is an elongated, conical capsule that is, in fact, the ovary of the flower. Okra pods are usually pale green but sometimes red, maroon, or even creamy white, and they're covered in fine down. The pod is comprised of five cavities containing ovules, or seeds. The degree of defined external ribbing depends on the variety. The heirloom variety Emerald is smooth and round, for example, while the external ribs of Eagle Pass are exceptionally well defined.

SEEDS

Each okra pod contains numerous smooth, white to dark brown, solid-colored or striated seeds. A 3-inch pod contains about 30–40 seeds. During the Civil War, when coffee was scarce and expensive due to the northern blockade, okra seeds were roasted, ground, and used as a coffee substitute. Having tried this in the interest of historical research, I will only say that this Confederate experiment seems to have been as much a failure as secession.

Okra seeds are the richest part of the pod, which has a high protein and fat content. The protein content of the seeds can be as high as 50 percent, depending on the variety. The seeds have huge potential as a source of oil, as coagulants, and for medical remedies that have yet to be exploited. There's a great deal of online chat about okra seeds being used in diabetes prevention and maintenance, but this claim has not yet been sanctioned by traditional medical authorities.

Where Okra Grows and Varieties

There are fifty species of wild and cultivated okra around the world. (As an okra missionary, I feel compelled to start checking each one off my list.) According to the U.S. Department of Agriculture, okra grows best in zones 4a through 11 in the United States. Okra is grown commercially in India, Turkey, Iran, West Africa, Yugoslavia, Bangladesh, Afghanistan, Pakistan, Burma, Japan, Malaysia, Brazil, Ghana, Ethiopia, Cyprus, and the United States, especially in the South and California. One acre of okra plants usually produces 200–250 bushels of okra, or approximately 600–750 pounds. That's a lot of gumbo.

"Open-pollinated," "self-pollinated," "heirloom," and "hybrid" are terms you'll hear often when buying seeds for your garden. "Open-pollinated" means the plant is pollinated by natural forces (such as wind or insects) without human intervention. "Self-pollinated" means the plant is fertilized by its own pollen. Okra is self-pollinating and produces flowers that contain both male and female parts. Problems occur when insects bring in other types of plant pollen, such as from other cultivars of okra, leading to cross-pollination. So be aware that if you grow several types of open-pollinated okra, they may crossbreed or cross-pollinate.

Quite a few heirloom okra varieties are now on the market, as well as those passed down through families. I love the names: Beck's Big Buck and Hill Country Red are so evocative. Some people consider heirlooms to be any vegetable cultivars that have been grown by people for a certain minimum number of years. According to Lynn Coulter's *Gardening with Heirloom Seeds*, some gardeners consider the minimum 50 years, whereas others won't consider anything less than a century or even 150 years. However, Coulter writes, the main consideration is that heirlooms are always open-pollinated, most can reproduce themselves from seed, and they have adapted over time to a specific climate and soil.

A hybrid is the offspring of two different varieties of plants produced through human manipulation for specific genetic characteristics. Many organic gardeners are wary of the term "hybrid" because they think hybrid seeds have been developed by an unnatural process in a laboratory. So it's important to distinguish between hybrids and GMOs, or genetically modified organisms. GMO seeds are altered in a laboratory using molecular genetic-engineering techniques, such as gene cloning or protein engineering. Hybrid varieties have simply been cross-pollinated by hand. The seeds from hybrid plants won't produce plants identical to the parent plant. That's why hybrids are not recommended for gardeners who plan to save seeds.

Increasingly popular heirloom varieties certainly have more diversity, but there's definitely a place for hybrids in the okra garden. Hybrids are developed to create, in a way, a super okra from two different varieties that possess the most desirable size, flavor, development, disease resistance, etc.

Seed companies that sell heirloom okra varieties include Southern Exposure Seed Exchange, Seed Savers Exchange, Baker Creek Heirloom Seed, and Sustainable Seed Company. For hybrid varieties, take a look at Burpee or Park Seed catalogs. You can also find Bonnie Plant hybrid seedlings at your local big-box hardware and home centers.

Here's a sampling of the diverse varieties of heirloom and hybrid okra to consider.

HEIRLOOMS

* *Alabama Red* grows 5–7 feet tall and produces an abundance of chunky red and green pods. Pods are ready to pick 75 days after seeds are sown.
* *Beck's Big Buck* is a German heirloom from Malcolm Beck of San Antonio, Texas. The 6-foot-tall plants produce an abundance of large, fat, tender, fluted pods. Uniquely, young pods easily snap off the plants when they're ready to be picked. Pods are ready for harvest in 75 days.
* *Bowling Red Okra* plants grow 7–8 feet tall and have deep red stems. The okra is long, slim, and red and green in color. According to Southern Exposure Seed Exchange, the Bowling family of Virginia has grown this heirloom since the 1920s. It's ready for harvest in 55 days.

* *Emerald* is a variety that was used by the Campbell Soup Company in the 1950s. The 5–8-foot-tall plants produce 6–8-inch round, smooth deep green pods. Emerald is ready for harvest in 50–75 days.
* *Hill Country Red* is a red and green plant that grows to 6 feet tall and produces fat, round, ribbed reddish-green pods. This Texas heirloom is a high producer, exceptionally drought tolerant, and ready for harvest in 64 days.
* *Jing Orange* is an Asian variety that grows up to 6 feet tall with red stems and green leaves. The pods are actually red, not orange, and are tender at 6–7 inches long. It's drought tolerant, productive, and ready for harvest in 60 days.
* *Perkins Mammoth Long Pod* is aptly named as it grows to a height of 6–10 feet and produces up to 16-inch-long bright green pods. Okra is ready for harvest in 60 days.
* *Red Burgundy* plants have deep red stems, leaf veins, and pods. The plants average 4 feet in height and produce narrow, spineless pods that remain tender nearly to their mature length of 7–8 inches. This okra can be harvested early at 49 days.
* *Red Velvet* is a red heirloom okra variety with bright rhubarb-colored pods, deep red stems, and green leaves. The plants grow 5 feet tall, and the pods are best when 3–5 inches long. This variety is ready for harvest in 70 days.
* *Star of David* is an eastern Mediterranean heirloom. It grows 7 feet tall or higher and produces fat, round pods. Okra is ready for harvest in 60–75 days.
* *Stewart's Zeebest* plants are bushy and 6–8 feet tall. The long, slender, curving pods are ribless and are said to remain tender even up to 8 inches long. Okra is ready for harvest in 77 days.
* *Vidrine's Midget Cowhorn* is an heirloom dwarf okra from St. Landry Parish, Louisiana. The 3-foot-tall plants produce pale green pods up to 15 inches long. "Cowhorn" refers to the fact that the long pods curl and twist like the horns of a cow.

* *Annie Oakley* is a spineless variety that can be planted fairly close together. The tapered, slender pods remain tender when mature for longer than some other okras. Annie Oakley pods are ready for harvest in 50 days.
* *Annie Oakley II* plants grow 4–5 feet tall and produce 2–3 times the yields of open-pollinated heirloom varieties. Annie Oakley II is well adapted for the cooler climates and shorter growing seasons of the Upper South and North. This hybrid is ready for harvest in 50 days.
* *Chant* grows to 5 feet in height. The pods are 5–6 inches long and are ready for harvest in 55 days.
* *Clemson Spineless* was introduced in 1939 and accounts for the majority of both commercial and home planting. The plants grow to about 4 feet high and produce an abundance of dark green, slightly grooved, straight, spineless, pointed pods. Pods are ready to pick about 56 days after seeds are sown.
* *Green Cajun Delight* is very productive and has tender dark green pods. An All-American Seed Winner, it has plants that are of medium height at 4–6 feet. It's an early variety, ready for harvest in 49 days.

Gardening Tips

If you just can't wait to get that okra in the dirt, start the seeds indoors in peat pots under full light 3–4 weeks before the last spring frost date. Be warned, however, that okra doesn't transplant very well—I've learned this the hard way. Or you can also start okra directly in your garden 3–4 weeks before the last spring frost date, as long as you cover the plants with a cold frame until the weather warms up. Some gardeners soak the seeds before planting to improve germination. This may help, but it also may kill the seedlings if the soil is too cold. The optimum soil temperature for seed germination is 70° to 95°. According to the Clemson University Extension Service, the preferred method to improve germination is to freeze the seeds before planting, which breaks the hard seed coat.

Plant okra in full sun—8–10 hours a day—for best productivity, and space the rows 3 feet apart to account for its wide root system. Make sure to position these large, tall plants in your garden where they won't shade out smaller plants. Sow seeds 1 inch deep and 4–6 inches apart within each row. When the seedlings are several inches tall, thin the row so the remaining plants are spaced roughly 1½–2 feet apart. I always dislike thinning out my plant babies, but the survivors are more likely to grow better as a result.

Okra grows best in loamy, sandy soil with good drainage and a pH between 5.8 and 6.5. Soil-testing kits are available at garden-supply stores. Your local County Cooperative Extension office will also test your soil sample for pH and nutrient levels at no charge or for a small fee. The soil analysis usually takes a few weeks and includes detailed results and suggested amendments specific to your area.

Okra thrives in hot, dry conditions; however, watering may be needed during the peak heat of the summer or an extended dry period. Adequate moisture is especially important during flowering and pod development. Thorough watering, preferably with a soaker hose or a drip irrigation tape, once every 7–10 days with about 1 inch of water is advisable during extended dry periods. If you use a sprinkler system, water in the morning so the leaves dry before dark. According to the University of Georgia College of Agriculture and Environmental Sciences, weed control is important, especially when the plants are small. Use a layer of organic mulch 2–3 inches thick to conserve moisture and control weeds.

Okra plants continue to flower and fruit for an indefinite time, depending on the variety, season, and soil moisture and fertility. In fact, regular harvesting stimulates production, so much so that it may be necessary to harvest every day. When you're harvesting, check very carefully among the leaves and branches for pods. Okra goes from petite and edible to pithy and inedible practically overnight. If a few pods slip by you and grow into giants, prune them to keep them from exhausting the plant. Also, when harvesting okra, it's best to use a paring knife or a pair of scissors to cut the pods from the stalks instead of pulling them off the plants. The plants will continue to produce until killed by frost.

To save the seeds for the next season, it's best to let the pods dry on the plant. However, don't wait too long or you may find yourself, literally, with an okra explosion. Okra belongs to a category of plants known as "explosive spreaders," meaning the fruits explode at maturity and shoot the seeds several feet away from the mother plant. The seeds of okra pods may spread up to 2–3 yards!

Pests and Diseases

Ants often seek out the sweet, sticky sap that comes off of okra pods and flowers, but they aren't actually harmful to the plant. The insects found on okra vary, but flea, Japanese, and blister beetles are most common. Flea beetles chew small holes in the leaves, and Japanese beetles can quickly make a plant a virtual skeleton. Seek treatment at your local garden store. There are both organic and chemical methods for dealing with these pests, and you can always pick them off and dispose of them by hand. The more serious okra diseases include stem blight and wilt. A combination of crop rotation and good soil management is important for controlling these diseases. Tender young seedlings are also susceptible to root-decaying diseases. This problem is more prevalent when the crop is planted in wet, cold soil. Another potential problem is the rotting of the small pods immediately after the flowers drop. Planting the crop in full sun, spacing plants properly, and providing good air movement through the plants will help minimize this problem.

Root-knot nematodes are microscopic parasitic worms that can cause serious damage to an okra crop. They are most often a problem in sandy and sandy-loam soils and are found mostly in hot climates with short winters, so the South is teed-up for the pest. According to the Clemson University Extension Service, if a plant seems stunted, you should pull it out of the ground and check for galls or knots on the roots. If you find knots, nematicides are not suggested for the home gardener, as they're expensive and highly toxic. An effective nematode-control program should include crop rotation and increasing the organic matter in the sandy soil by adding compost.

Choosing Okra

You've planted, tended, and watered. Finally, you have okra! Choose young pods, usually no longer than 4 inches in length, depending on the variety. There's a reason the pods are called ladyfingers—for most plants, seek out pods smaller than a lady's finger since the larger pods are generally tough and fibrous. Okra pods should be firm, unblemished, and brightly colored. Green is most common, but you may also find red or deep burgundy varieties, even pale green, almost white, at local farmers' markets. Avoid limp, bruised, blemished, or moldy pods.

Frozen okra is an acceptable substitute and is most often found in cut pieces about ½ inch long, both plain and breaded for frying. It's less common to find whole-pod frozen okra, especially outside of the Southeast, but it's available.

When to Purchase Okra

The peak season for okra in the Southeast is May through October, although I've found it available at Indian markets nearly year-round. The primary growing season is, of course, summer, but okra is produced ten months out of the year in Florida. Okra is imported from Mexico, the West Indies, and Central and South America during the winter months. Okra doesn't hold up well after harvest. As a cook and food writer, I encourage people to eat locally and seasonally. The food will simply taste better.

How to Store Okra

Store unwashed okra in a paper bag in the refrigerator for up to three days. If you have a bumper crop, you might want to consider freezing it. According to the National Center for Home Preservation, the smooth varieties freeze better than the ridged varieties because they don't split as readily. Before freezing okra, it should be blanched to slow or stop the action of enzymes, which cause a loss of flavor, color, and texture. Blanching also brightens the color, helps prevent the loss of vitamins, and softens the pods so they're easier to pack.

To freeze okra, select tender young pods and separate them into small pods (4 inches or under) and large pods (so you can package them separately and cook each size more evenly). Wash them under cold running water, then trim the stem ends. Working with about a pound at a time, blanch the pods in a large pot of boiling salted water for 3–4 minutes, depending on the size. Remove with a slotted spoon and shock in ice water to set the color and stop the cooking. Drain well. A word of advice: if you're putting up lots of okra, freshen both the cooking water and the ice-water bath fairly often since the water can become a bit slimy.

Once the pods have been blanched and drained, arrange them in a single layer on a baking sheet either whole or sliced into ½-inch pieces and then place the baking sheet uncovered in the freezer. Once the okra pieces are frozen, put them in an airtight container or plastic freezer bag. Because the okra was frozen in a single layer first, the pieces will stay loose and you can take out just the amount you need.

How to Prepare Okra for Cooking

To prepare okra for cooking, wash the fresh pods under cold running water and pat dry. Trim the stem ends, taking care not to pierce the pods if using them whole. For faster cooking, cut the pods crosswise into ½-inch pieces. Some cooks, like my mother and grandmother, cut the entire stem cap off the pod. Many of the Mediterranean recipes I found while doing research for this book call for peeling the tough skin off of the conical cap, leaving the okra flesh below. I prefer to leave the entire cap on the okra, simply snipping the stem end before cooking to create a fresher, more tender cut than when the okra pod was harvested from the plant. I think the cap is pretty, and the whole pod is quite elegant, far more attractive than a decapitated okra pod.

Top Ten Slime-Busting Tips

The proverbial elephant in the room with okra is the slime, also known as mucilage or roping. The mucilage is a type of soluble digestible fiber. In the plant, it aids in water storage, prevents the seed from drying out, and assists with seed germination. Some folks don't mind the slime; others consider it the downfall of okra. Here are my top ten cooking tips to bust the slime for those who don't like it:

1. Choose small pods.
2. Wash and dry okra thoroughly. Very, very thoroughly.
3. Don't cut okra into pieces; cook whole pods. Some of my recipes call for cut okra. To reduce the slime factor, adjust the recipe and cooking time to use whole pods.
4. If cutting okra into pieces, wipe your knife on a kitchen towel between each slice so as not to spread the slime.
5. Add an acid like tomato, lemon juice, vinegar, or wine when cooking.
6. Overcooking produces more slime, so don't overcook okra.
7. Don't crowd the pan when cooking, as the steam will produce more slime.
8. Cook okra quickly at high heat.
9. Don't cover okra while cooking.
10. If okra is a component of a recipe, you can cook it separately, then add it to the finished dish.

Health and Nutritional Information

Okra is a very healthy food and a potent antioxidant. It's low in calories: 1 cup of raw okra has only about 30 calories and an impressive 66 percent of the recommended daily allowance of vitamin K. Vitamin K is known as the "clotting vitamin," as it's necessary for blood to clot. Some studies suggest that it also helps maintain strong bones in the elderly.

Okra is also low in sodium, fat-free, and cholesterol-free. Okra is high in calcium; vitamins C, A, and B6; protein; folate; manganese; and magnesium. It's also a good source of riboflavin, niacin, phosphorus, potassium, zinc, copper, thiamin, and folate. It's high in dietary fiber, with over 5 grams per 3½-ounce serving. No doubt about it—okra is good and good for you.

Okra may be beneficial for people suffering renal colic, typically caused by kidney stones. And due to its high iodine content, it may be useful for those suffering from goiter, or an enlargement of the thyroid gland. Experiments are being conducted to discover if okra can help control blood sugar absorption, as claimed in natural-remedy circles. Last and perhaps most famously, okra prevents gas and is a very effective natural laxative due to its high fiber content.

Around the World

As with all of the Savor the South® cookbooks, *Okra* shares a wealth of information about a classic southern ingredient. I've chosen to include both southern and global recipes in this book in order to see what an iconic southern ingredient like okra might look like in someone else's skillet.

You'll find fifty recipes in this book. The first section includes recipes from the southern kitchen that range from old-fashioned to chef-chic. The recipes in the second section span the globe.

I've maintained as much authenticity as possible in recipes from the various cuisines. Those recipes have been reviewed by experts in the respective cuisines and slightly adapted for the American kitchen. After all, both the South and the United States are diverse melting pots. Ethnic markets of many cultures can now be found in shopping centers and strip malls across the country, making it possible to obtain once hard-to-find ingredients. And, of course, nearly any ingredient is available with a handy search engine and online ordering.

Whether you're an avid okra lover or just now exploring the joys of okra, I'm certain you'll find recipes here that you and your family will savor.

Bon appétit, y'all!

Southern Okra Recipes

In the United States, okra is widely perceived as solely a southern vegetable. You're highly unlikely to find okra on the menu in Napa or in one of the temples of molecular gastronomy in Chicago. I did see it as a component of a fancy salad at a Michelin-starred restaurant in New York City, but the poor pod was nearly unrecognizable. When I have seen it at farmers' markets in New England, sadly most of the pods are too large or too long. Farmers outside of the South aren't certain how to grow it and haven't had to contend with the prolific volume produced, and nonsouthern consumers don't know how to cook it. Okra may be slowly making its way out of the South, but very, very slowly—at the same glacial pace as a honey-butter southern drawl. The following recipes consist of a few versions of fried okra, then we move into pickled okra, try a few more upscale roasted okra recipes, take a dip in the land of gumbo and pilaus, then finish up with the classic okra and tomatoes. Down-home cooking and southern white-tablecloth restaurants both embrace okra. After a taste of this chapter, I'm sure you will too.

Southern-Style Fried Okra

Frying can be messy if you aren't set up in an efficient fashion. Set up a frying center that lets you move easily from marinating the okra to coating it in the dry ingredients to placing it in the hot oil. Only dredge what you can fry at one time: don't coat all of the okra and then start frying since the coating will become dense and gummy on the later batches. Lastly, don't fry too much okra at once or the oil will cool down and the okra won't cook properly.

MAKES 4–6 SERVINGS

---

1 pound okra, stem ends trimmed, cut into ½-inch pieces
1 cup buttermilk
Coarse kosher salt and freshly ground black pepper
1 cup all-purpose flour
1 cup medium-grind cornmeal (not self-rising)
3 cups peanut oil, plus more if needed

Line a plate with paper towels and set it next to the stovetop. Combine the okra and buttermilk in a bowl. Season with salt and pepper. Combine the flour and cornmeal in a second bowl. Using a slotted spoon, remove a large spoonful of okra from the liquid, letting the excess buttermilk run back into the bowl. Place the okra in the flour mixture and toss to coat.

Meanwhile, heat the oil in a large cast-iron skillet over medium-high heat until it reaches 350° on a deep-fat thermometer. (You can also test the heat by sprinkling a bit of flour into the hot oil to see whether it bubbles.) When the oil is hot, add the coated okra to the skillet.

Cook until brown and crisp, 3–5 minutes. Using a slotted spoon, transfer the cooked okra to the prepared plate. Repeat with the remaining okra. Season with salt and pepper. Serve immediately.

Shoestring Fried Okra

"Crispy strips of deep-fried goodness" is the best way to describe Shoestring Fried Okra. Because it's best straight out of the oil, it can't really be made ahead. The bonus is, it turns the kitchen into a party.

MAKES 4–6 SERVINGS

1 pound okra, stem ends trimmed
¼ cup all-purpose flour
Coarse kosher salt and freshly ground black pepper
4 cups peanut oil, plus more if needed

Line a baking sheet with paper towels and set it next to the stovetop. Using a very sharp knife, slice each okra pod in half lengthwise. Then cut each half into ⅛-inch julienne strips. Place a handful of okra slices in a bowl and sprinkle with flour. Season with salt and pepper. Toss until the okra slices are well coated with flour.

Meanwhile, heat the oil in a large cast-iron skillet over medium-high heat until it registers 375° on a deep-fat thermometer. When the oil is hot, add the coated okra. Cook, turning as needed, until the okra is golden brown, 3–5 minutes. Using a slotted spoon, transfer the okra to the prepared baking sheet. Season with salt and pepper. Repeat with the remaining okra. Serve immediately.

Double-Dipped Fried Okra

My friend and colleague, Chef Marvin Woods, taught me this recipe. Frying whole small okra pods gives this dish a completely different flavor and texture from traditional thinly sliced fried okra. One taste of this crunchy treat and you'll agree that it's the one time it's okay to double dip.

MAKES 4–6 SERVINGS

1 pound okra, stem ends trimmed

1 quart buttermilk

1 cup all-purpose flour

3/4 cup fine cornmeal (not self-rising)

1/2 teaspoon chili powder

1/2 teaspoon garlic powder

1/2 teaspoon onion powder

1/2 teaspoon cayenne pepper

Coarse kosher salt and freshly ground black pepper

2 cups vegetable oil, plus more if needed

Line a baking sheet with paper towels and set it next to the stovetop. Combine the okra and buttermilk in a bowl. In a shallow bowl or pie plate, stir together the flour, cornmeal, chili powder, garlic powder, onion powder, and cayenne pepper. Season heartily with salt and pepper.

Using a slotted spoon, remove a few pods of okra from the buttermilk, letting the excess buttermilk run back into the bowl. Place the okra in the flour mixture and toss to lightly coat. Transfer to a sieve or colander and shake to remove any excess flour. Then return the okra to the buttermilk and repeat the procedure for a second coating.

Meanwhile, heat the oil in a large cast-iron skillet over medium-high heat until it registers 350° on a deep-fat thermometer. When the oil is hot, using tongs or a slotted spoon, add the coated okra. Cook, turning as needed, until the okra is evenly browned on all sides, 3–5 minutes. Using a slotted spoon, transfer the okra to the prepared baking sheet. Season with salt and pepper. Repeat with the remaining okra. Serve immediately.

Oven-Fried Okra

Let's face it, there's really nothing like fried okra, but this oven-fried version comes darn close. I prefer to use organic canola cooking spray. It has little flavor, a high smoke point for high-heat cooking, and no aftertaste like some cooking sprays seem to have.

MAKES 4–6 SERVINGS

---

1 cup fine cornmeal (not self-rising)

¼ teaspoon cayenne pepper, or to taste

Coarse kosher salt and freshly ground black pepper

½ cup buttermilk

1 large egg, lightly beaten

1 pound okra, stem ends trimmed, cut into ¾-inch pieces

Cooking spray

Place a rimmed baking sheet in the oven. Preheat the oven to 450°.

Combine the cornmeal and cayenne pepper in a shallow dish. Season heartily with salt and pepper.

Whisk together the buttermilk and egg in a large bowl. Add the okra and season with salt and pepper. Stir to combine and set aside to marinate, about 3 minutes.

Using a slotted spoon, remove the okra from the buttermilk and add it to the cornmeal mixture. Dredge the okra in the cornmeal mixture. Remove the baking sheet from the oven and spray it with cooking spray. Place the okra on the heated pan and lightly coat it with additional cooking spray. Bake for 25 minutes, stirring once. Stir and spray again. Cook an additional 10–12 minutes. Remove from the oven and season with salt and pepper. Serve immediately.

Spicy Quick-Pickled Okra

Southerners are almost as fond of pickling as we are of frying. Submerging fresh produce in vinegar or a combination of sugar and vinegar once guaranteed that we would have vegetables to eat in the winter months. While this quick pickle is meant to be enjoyed within several weeks, okra also responds very well to long-term pickling. The vinegar virtually eliminates the slime factor. I like to use these crisp, spicy pods instead of olives in southern-style martinis.

MAKES 4 PINTS

4 small dried chili peppers, such as chilies de árbol or bird's eye

2 teaspoons brown mustard seeds

1 teaspoon whole black peppercorns

8 garlic cloves, peeled

2 pounds medium okra, stem ends trimmed

4 cups distilled white vinegar

2 cups water

2 tablespoons pickling salt (see Note)

Place 1 chili, ½ teaspoon mustard seeds, ¼ teaspoon peppercorns, and 2 garlic cloves in each of 4 sterilized pint jars. Divide the okra evenly among the jars, placing the pods vertically with stems alternating up and down.

In a medium saucepan over medium heat, bring the vinegar, water, and salt to a boil. Carefully pour the boiling mixture over the okra in the jars, leaving ¼ inch of headroom between the liquid and the top of the jar. Seal the lids. Let cool to room temperature. Store in the refrigerator for up to 6 weeks.

NOTE ❋ Pickling salt is a pure fine-granulated salt, with no added preservatives or free-flowing agents. It dissolves quickly and produces a clear brine, which is why it's the preferred salt for pickling and canning.

Southern Sushi

My dear friend and fellow cookbook author Rebecca Lang shared this recipe with me. Okra, ham, and cream cheese are the southern lady's version of the holy trinity and are served at garden parties and bridge luncheons all across the South. I adore this little cocktail nibble.

MAKES ABOUT 40 ROLLS

1 (8-ounce) package cream cheese, at room temperature
1 tablespoon chopped chives
1 tablespoon chopped flat-leaf parsley
3 tablespoons finely diced sweet onion
1 (16-ounce) jar pickled okra, drained (about 18 okra pods)
⅓ pound thinly sliced Virginia ham (about 8 slices)

Combine the cream cheese, chives, parsley, and onion. Trim both ends off the okra pods. On a large cutting board, lay out each slice of ham. Spread about 2 tablespoons of the cream cheese mixture on each slice of ham, leaving a border of about ¼ inch.

On the long side of each ham slice, lay 2–3 okra pods, end to end, depending on the size of the ham slice. Roll the ham around the okra. Cover and chill the rolls for 3 hours, then slice them into 1-inch slices and serve.

Grilled Okra and Hot Peppers

Many recipes suggest soaking bamboo skewers in water to use on the grill. This never works very well for me, and I wind up with something that resembles kindling. My advice is to buy metal skewers and be done with it. This recipe is adapted from my book Basic to Brilliant, Y'all *and was chosen as one of* Food & Wine *magazine's favorite recipes of 2011.*

MAKES 4–6 SERVINGS

4 peppers, such as jalapeño, yellow hot, or banana peppers
1½ pounds okra, stem ends trimmed
1 tablespoon canola oil
Coarse kosher salt and freshly ground black pepper

Prepare a fire using about 5 pounds of charcoal and burn the coals until they're completely covered with a thin coating of light gray ash, 20–30 minutes. Spread the coals evenly over the bottom of the grill, position the grill rack above the coals, and heat until medium-hot (you've reached the right temperature when you can hold your hand 5 inches above the grill surface for no longer than 3 or 4 seconds). Or, for a gas grill, turn all burners to high, close the lid, and heat until very hot, 10–15 minutes.

Meanwhile, slice the peppers into coins about ¼ inch thick. Thread the okra pods crosswise onto the skewers, inserting slices of pepper between every other pod or so, depending on how much kick you want. Brush with the oil and season with salt and pepper. Transfer to the grill and cook until the okra is bright green and tender, 2–3 minutes per side. Remove from the grill and serve immediately.

Herb-Roasted Okra

The combination of lemon zest and herbs is fresh and light. If you want a bit of heat, try sprinkling crushed red pepper flakes or perhaps a more exotic pepper such as Aleppo or pimente d'Espelette over the okra.

MAKES 4–6 SERVINGS

1 pound okra, stem ends trimmed
4 mint sprigs, leaves only (about 12 leaves)
4 large basil leaves, freshly torn
1 onion, thinly sliced
2 garlic cloves, thinly sliced
Zest of 1 lemon
3 tablespoons extra-virgin olive oil
Coarse kosher salt and freshly ground black pepper

Preheat the oven to 375°. Line a rimmed baking sheet with a nonstick silicone liner.

Place the okra, mint, basil, onion, garlic, and lemon zest in a large bowl and drizzle over the olive oil. Season with salt and pepper; toss to coat. Transfer to the prepared baking sheet and roast until tender, about 20 minutes. Taste and adjust for seasoning with salt and pepper. Serve immediately.

Okra with Butter

This is the most simple and delicate of okra preparations; it's almost not a recipe. Choose very fresh, small pods, and just snip the very tip of the stem end, where it was attached to the plant, leaving the cap whole.

MAKES 4–6 SERVINGS

½ cup water
1 pound okra, stem ends trimmed
Coarse kosher salt and freshly ground black pepper
1 tablespoon unsalted butter

Heat the water in a medium saucepan over medium-high heat. Add the okra and season with salt and pepper. Cover and cook until bright green and just tender, about 6 minutes. Pour off the water. Add the butter and swirl to melt. Taste and adjust for seasoning with salt and pepper. Serve immediately.

Fresh Black-Eyed Peas and Okra

Black-eyed peas and okra very likely originated from the same region of Africa and journeyed together across the Atlantic. This simple combination belies the flavorful results. Serve this with a wedge of cornbread for a perfectly wonderful summer side dish. If you're unable to locate fresh peas, you can substitute frozen, but avoid canned ones as they're often too mushy and salty.

MAKES 4–6 SERVINGS

---

2 tablespoons olive oil

1 onion, finely chopped

1 large garlic clove, finely chopped

3 cups homemade chicken stock or reduced-fat, low-sodium chicken broth

2 small bay leaves, preferably fresh

2 cups freshly shelled black-eyed peas (about 1¾ pounds unshelled) or frozen black-eyed peas, thawed

Coarse kosher salt and freshly ground black pepper

1 pound okra, stem ends trimmed, cut into ½-inch pieces

¼ teaspoon crushed red pepper flakes, or to taste

Heat the olive oil in a large saucepan over medium heat. Add the onion and cook until soft and translucent, 3–5 minutes. Add the garlic and cook until fragrant, 45–60 seconds. Add the stock and bay leaves and bring to a boil. Add the peas and reduce the heat to simmer. Season with salt and pepper. Cook, uncovered and stirring occasionally, for 20 minutes. Add the okra and red pepper flakes. Simmer until tender, an additional 15 minutes. Remove the bay leaves. Taste and adjust for seasoning with salt and pepper. Serve immediately.

Round Steak and Okra Gumbo

Round steak is the cut of beef most often used for country-fried steak in the South. It's from the back leg of a cow, is quite lean, and can be very tough. It's often sold as steaks a little less than ½ inch thick. Even though I grew up eating gumbo in Louisiana, I wasn't familiar with beef gumbo until I started research for this book. This recipe is old-fashioned country cooking—inexpensive, filling, and really, really good.

MAKES 4–6 SERVINGS

1 pound beef round steak, sliced into 1-inch strips

Coarse kosher salt and freshly ground black pepper

4 tablespoons canola oil, divided

1 slice ham steak, about ½ inch thick, diced

2 tablespoons all-purpose flour

1 onion, finely chopped

1 quart homemade beef stock or reduced-fat, low-sodium beef broth, heated

1 pound okra, stem ends trimmed, finely chopped

Season the round steak with salt and pepper. Heat 2 tablespoons of the oil in a large heavy-bottomed pot until shimmering. Add the steak and ham. Cook until the steak is browned on both sides, 2–2½ minutes per side. Using a slotted spoon, remove the steak and ham to a plate.

Add the remaining 2 tablespoons of oil to the drippings in the pot. Add the flour and stir to combine. Cook until brown, about 5 minutes. Add the onion and cook until soft and translucent, 3–5 minutes. Return the browned meats to the pan and stir to combine. Then add the stock and okra and season with salt and pepper. Bring to a boil, then reduce the heat to simmer. Simmer, covered and stirring occasionally, until the meat is tender, about 1 hour. Taste and adjust for seasoning with salt and pepper. Serve immediately.

Gulf Coast Seafood Gumbo

Creole cooking is inextricably linked to the city of New Orleans, but the flavors of Creole food extend beyond Louisiana. Creole is the marriage of French-Canadian settlers, African slaves, and Native Americans. Okra is traditional in this rich and savory soup.

MAKES 6–8 SERVINGS

¾ cup peanut oil

1 cup all-purpose flour

1 onion, chopped

1 green bell pepper, seeded and chopped

1 red bell pepper, seeded and chopped

2 stalks celery, chopped

3 garlic cloves, finely chopped

1 pound okra, stem ends trimmed, cut into ¼-inch pieces

5 cups water or seafood stock

3 bay leaves, preferably fresh

3 thyme sprigs

2 teaspoons hot sauce, or to taste

Coarse kosher salt and freshly ground black pepper

1 pound large shrimp (21/25 count), peeled and deveined

1 pound lump crabmeat, picked through for cartilage and shell

2 dozen freshly shucked oysters, liquid reserved

3 tablespoons chopped flat-leaf parsley

2 scallions, chopped (white and tender green parts)

Cooked rice, for serving

Heat the oil in a heavy-bottomed pot over medium heat. Add the flour and stir to combine. Cook, stirring often, until the mixture is medium brown in color, like peanut butter, about 30 minutes. Add the onion, bell peppers, and celery. Cook, stirring, until the vegetables are wilted and lightly golden, about 5 minutes. Add the garlic and cook until fragrant, 45–60 seconds. Add the okra, water, bay leaves, thyme sprigs, and hot sauce; season with salt and pepper. Reduce the heat to medium-low, cover, and simmer for 45 minutes.

Add the shrimp and crabmeat and simmer until the shrimp turn pink, about 4 minutes. Add the oysters and their liquid and simmer until the edges of the oysters curl, about 2 minutes. Remove the bay leaves and thyme sprigs. Taste and adjust for seasoning with salt and pepper. Garnish with the parsley and scallions. Serve over rice.

Skillet-Roasted Okra and Shrimp

The flavors of this dish are bright and clean. Serve it atop a bowl of stone-ground grits for an exceptional combination, or for something even lighter, try it as a warm salad on a bed of arugula. When buying shrimp, look for firm shrimp with a mild, almost sweet scent. If there's any trace of ammonia, it's a sign that the shrimp are no longer fresh.

MAKES 4–6 SERVINGS

3 tablespoons olive oil, divided
½ pound okra, stem ends trimmed, halved lengthwise
1 pint grape tomatoes
1 pound large shrimp (21/25 count), peeled and deveined
½ teaspoon crushed red pepper flakes, or to taste
3 garlic cloves, finely chopped
2 tablespoons chopped flat-leaf parsley
Coarse kosher salt and freshly ground black pepper

Heat 1 tablespoon of the olive oil in a large cast-iron skillet over medium-high heat. Add the okra and cook until lightly browned, 4–5 minutes. Transfer to a bowl.

Heat another tablespoon of the olive oil in the same skillet. Add the tomatoes. Cook over medium-high heat, stirring occasionally, until the skins are charred, about 3 minutes. Transfer to the bowl with the okra.

Heat the remaining tablespoon of olive oil in the same skillet over high heat until shimmering. Add the shrimp and red pepper flakes and cook until the shrimp turn pink, 2–3 minutes. Add the garlic and cook until fragrant, 45–60 seconds. Stir in the okra and tomatoes. Cook for 1–2 minutes or until thoroughly heated. Add the parsley and season with salt and pepper. Serve immediately.

Limpin' Susan

Legend has it that Limpin' Susan was the wife of Hoppin' John. Hoppin' John is a dish made of rice, pork, and black-eyed peas served throughout the year but traditionally always on New Year's Day. Little is known about the origin of the names Hoppin' John and Limpin' Susan, which consists of rice, bacon, and okra. Both are one-pot, inexpensive meals.

MAKES 4–6 SERVINGS

3 strips lean bacon, cut into lardons (see Note)
¾ pound okra, stem ends trimmed, cut into ¼-inch pieces
1 onion, chopped
1 cup long-grain rice
1½ cups water
Coarse kosher salt and freshly ground black pepper

Preheat the oven to 350°.

Heat a large saucepan over medium-high heat. Add the bacon and cook until crispy, about 3 minutes. Add the okra and onion and sauté, stirring occasionally, until the onion is translucent and the okra is tender, 3–5 minutes. Add the rice and water. Season with 1 teaspoon of salt and pepper to taste.

Bring to a boil over medium-high heat. Cover with a tight-fitting lid and transfer to the oven. Cook until the liquid is absorbed and the rice is tender, about 27 minutes. Remove from the oven and let stand, covered, for 5 minutes before serving. Taste and adjust for seasoning with salt and pepper. Serve immediately.

NOTE ❋ Bacon lardons are matchstick-size pieces of bacon, though strictly speaking, a lardon is a long strip of fat sewn into lean meat with a larding needle (*lardoire*) to keep the meat moist and flavorful during cooking.

Carolina Crab and Shrimp Pilau

"Pilau" and "perloo" are Low Country terms for one-pot rice-based dishes that are essentially pilafs. The basic technique for making pilaf is pretty straightforward: The rice is toasted in fat, then simmered in liquid, and finally removed from the heat to steam.

MAKES 6 SERVINGS

1 tablespoon canola oil

1 onion, chopped

2 garlic cloves, finely chopped

$\frac{1}{2}$ pound okra, stem ends trimmed, cut into $\frac{1}{2}$-inch pieces

$\frac{1}{2}$ red bell pepper, seeded and diced

$\frac{1}{2}$ teaspoon Old Bay seasoning

$\frac{1}{2}$ teaspoon cayenne pepper, or to taste

1$\frac{1}{2}$ cups long-grain white rice

Coarse kosher salt and freshly ground black pepper

2$\frac{1}{2}$ cups water or seafood stock

1 thyme sprig

1 pound large shrimp (21/25 count), peeled and deveined

8 ounces jumbo lump crabmeat, picked through for cartilage and shell

Heat the oil in a large skillet over medium-high heat until shimmering. Add the onion and cook until soft and translucent, 3–5 minutes. Add the garlic and cook until fragrant, 45–60 seconds. Add the okra and red bell pepper and cook until bright, another 2 minutes. Add the Old Bay, cayenne pepper, and rice; stir to combine. Cook, stirring constantly, until the rice is coated and lightly toasted. Season with 1 teaspoon of salt and pepper to taste. Add the water and thyme sprig and stir to combine. Bring to a boil over medium-high heat. Reduce the heat to simmer. Cover and cook for 15 minutes.

Add the shrimp and crab and stir to combine. Continue to cook for an additional 5 minutes. Remove from the heat and let stand, covered, for 5 minutes. Remove the thyme sprig. Taste and adjust for seasoning with salt and pepper. Serve immediately.

Southern Ratatouille

Don't bother with this recipe unless it's summer and you can make it with fresh eggplant and squash and the best tomatoes, preferably heirloom. Otherwise, you'll be disappointed. Heirloom tomatoes, varieties passed down through generations by farmers and gardeners the world over, come in all shapes, sizes, colors, and tastes. If you can't find heirlooms, just make sure to use the freshest and ripest tomatoes from your garden or market.

MAKES 4–6 SERVINGS

2 tablespoons olive oil

1 onion, chopped

2 garlic cloves, finely chopped

1 large eggplant, cut into ¾-inch cubes

2 yellow squash, cut into 1-inch cubes

Coarse kosher salt and freshly ground black pepper

¾ cup water

½ red bell pepper, seeded and chopped

½ poblano pepper, seeded and chopped

3 tomatoes, seeded and chopped

1 pound okra, stem ends trimmed

1 teaspoon chopped thyme

½ cup chopped basil

Heat the olive oil over medium heat in a large heavy-bottomed saucepan with a tight-fitting lid. Add the onion and cook, stirring occasionally, until translucent, 3–5 minutes. Add the garlic and cook until fragrant, 45–60 seconds. Stir in the eggplant and squash; season generously with salt and pepper. Add the water, cover, and simmer, stirring once, until the vegetables are beginning to soften, about 5 minutes. Stir in the red bell pepper and poblano pepper; simmer, covered, until softened, about 5 minutes. Stir in the tomatoes, okra, and thyme; bring to a boil.

Decrease the heat to medium-low. Partially cover and simmer, stirring often, until the vegetables are tender, 15–20 minutes. Remove from the heat. Just before serving, stir in the basil. Taste and adjust for seasoning with salt and pepper. Serve warm, at room temperature, or cold.

Fresh Summer Vegetable Succotash with Herbs

Succotash has many variations, but the one common theme is that it traditionally contains corn and beans. If butter beans are not available, I often substitute shelled edamame. This dish and maque choux are kissing cousins, both rumored to have originally been Native American dishes.

MAKES 6 SERVINGS

---

2 cups shelled fresh butter beans (about 1½ pounds unshelled beans) or frozen butter beans, thawed

Coarse kosher salt and freshly ground black pepper

¼ pound small Yukon Gold potatoes, halved

2 tablespoons canola oil, divided

2 tablespoons unsalted butter, divided

1 onion, chopped

½ pound okra, stem ends trimmed, cut into ½-inch pieces

2 cups sweet corn kernels, plus milky liquid from scraping the cobs (from about 4 ears corn)

2 small zucchini, diced

¼ cup mixed chopped herbs, such as basil, tarragon, and parsley

---

To cook the beans, place them in a pot and cover with cold water. Bring to a boil over high heat and season with salt and pepper; decrease the heat to low. Simmer until tender, about 30 minutes for fresh beans, less for frozen. Drain well.

To cook the potatoes, place them in a second saucepan and cover by 1 inch with cold water; season with salt. Bring to a boil over high heat and then decrease the heat to low and simmer until the potatoes are just tender, about 20 minutes. Drain in a colander. (Alternatively, you can microwave these for a few minutes, depending on the power level of your microwave, to parcook them just to tender.)

In a large heavy-bottomed skillet, heat 1 tablespoon of the oil and 1 tablespoon of the butter over high heat until the foam subsides. Add the drained potatoes and season with salt and pepper. Cook, stirring infrequently, until nicely crusted, 8–10 minutes. Transfer the potatoes to a bowl and keep warm.

Heat the remaining 1 tablespoon oil and 1 tablespoon butter in the same skillet over medium-high heat; add the onion, okra, and corn. Cook, stirring, until crisp-tender, about 5 minutes. Add the zucchini and cook until tender, about 5 minutes. Stir in the butter beans and potatoes; cook, stirring, until heated through. Add the herbs. Taste and adjust for seasoning with salt and pepper. Serve hot, warm, or cold.

Okra Maque Choux

Maque choux, pronounced "mock shoe," is believed to be a dish taught to the Cajuns by Native Americans. The technique of scraping the milky liquid from very fresh corn cobs contributes to its creaminess. You can use butter or bacon grease instead of canola oil if you're feeling a bit indulgent. My grandmother always had a tin of bacon drippings next to the stovetop, a sight less common now in southern kitchens. It usually takes 2–3 slices of bacon to produce 1 tablespoon of bacon grease, depending on the brand.

MAKES 4–6 SERVINGS

---

1 tablespoon canola oil, butter, or bacon grease
1 sweet onion, chopped
1 red bell pepper, seeded and chopped
2 garlic cloves, very finely chopped
3 cups sweet corn kernels, plus milky liquid from scraping
   the cobs (from about 6 ears corn)
½ pound okra, stem ends trimmed, cut into ¼-inch pieces
1 tomato, seeded and chopped
Coarse kosher salt and freshly ground black pepper

Heat the oil in a large skillet over medium-high heat until shimmering. Add the onion and red bell pepper and cook until soft and translucent, 3–5 minutes. Add the garlic and cook until fragrant, 45–60 seconds. Add the corn and milky liquid, okra, and tomato; season with salt and pepper. Cook, stirring occasionally, until the vegetables are tender, about 10 minutes. Taste and adjust for seasoning with salt and pepper. Serve immediately.

Old-School Okra and Tomatoes

To prevent okra from becoming too slimy, first and foremost, don't overcook it. When okra is cooked to just tender, it's fresh and crisp, not "ropey." Another technique is to cook okra with an acid. This recipe uses both tomato and a bit of red wine for best results.

MAKES 4–6 SERVINGS

2 tablespoons canola oil
1 onion, chopped
1 garlic clove, finely chopped
½ cup dry red wine
1 pound okra, stem ends trimmed, cut into ½-inch pieces
4 tomatoes, seeded and chopped
3 thyme sprigs
2 bay leaves, preferably fresh
Coarse kosher salt and freshly ground black pepper

Heat the oil in a sauté pan over medium heat. Add the onion and cook, stirring until soft and translucent, 3–5 minutes. Add the garlic and cook until fragrant, 45–60 seconds. Add the red wine and cook until reduced by half.

Add the okra, tomatoes, thyme sprigs, and bay leaves. Season with salt and pepper. Cover and reduce the heat to a low simmer. Cook, stirring occasionally, until the vegetables are tender, 12–14 minutes. Remove the thyme sprigs and bay leaves. Taste and adjust for seasoning with salt and pepper. Serve immediately.

Chef-Style Stewed Okra and Tomatoes

"Chef-style" simply means taking a bit more care to maintain the integrity of the ingredients, cooking them separately and marrying them together at the end. This recipe was inspired by a recipe in Chef John Besh's My New Orleans: The Cookbook. *Make sure the carrot is very finely grated—I use a microplane—so it just melts away, leaving a hint of sweetness.*

MAKES 4–6 SERVINGS

---

1 pound okra, stem ends trimmed

1 tablespoon coarse kosher salt

1 tablespoon olive oil

3 large tomatoes, peeled, seeded, and chopped (see Cooking Tip)

3 garlic cloves, thinly sliced

1 carrot, very finely grated

$\frac{1}{2}$ teaspoon crushed red pepper flakes, or to taste

2 tablespoons chopped basil

Freshly ground black pepper

Cooked rice, for serving

Make an ice-water bath by filling a large bowl with ice and water. Line a plate with paper towels. Bring a large pot of salted water to a rolling boil over high heat. Add the okra and return to a boil. Cook until bright green, about 3 minutes. Drain the okra well in a colander, then set the colander with the okra in the ice-water bath (to set the color and stop the cooking), making sure the okra is submerged. Once cooled, drain the okra well and remove it to the prepared plate.

Meanwhile, heat the olive oil in a medium skillet over medium-high heat until shimmering. Add the tomatoes and garlic and cook, stirring occasionally, 2–3 minutes. Add the carrot and pepper flakes and cook, stirring occasionally, until thick and reduced, about 10 minutes.

Add the basil and okra and stir to combine. Reduce the heat slightly and cook for 3–4 minutes. Taste and adjust for seasoning with salt and pepper. Serve immediately over rice.

COOKING TIP ❋ To peel a tomato, using a sharp knife, score an "X" in the bottom of each tomato, being careful not to pierce too deeply into the flesh. Drop 1 or 2 at a time into a large pot of boiling water for 10 seconds and then place them in ice water to stop them from cooking. Using your fingers or a paring knife, remove the skin, being careful not to break the fruit. To seed a tomato, halve it horizontally. Then, working with 1 half at a time and squeezing slightly, insert your index finger into each pocket and remove the seeds.

Spicy Okra and Tomatoes

This recipe has subtle Indian influences, but it's not too far out of the box for folks who prefer tamer okra choices. To chop the canned tomatoes, simply snip away in the can with a pair of clean kitchen scissors instead of making a mess on your cutting board.

MAKES 4–6 SERVINGS

1/4 cup canola oil

1 pound okra, stem ends trimmed, cut into 1/2-inch pieces

1 onion, chopped

2 garlic cloves, very finely chopped

1/4-inch coin of ginger, peeled and very finely chopped

2 teaspoons ground cumin

2 teaspoons ground coriander

1/4 teaspoon cayenne pepper, or to taste

1/4 teaspoon ground turmeric

1 (28-ounce) can whole tomatoes, chopped, with juices

Coarse kosher salt and freshly ground black pepper

2 tablespoons chopped cilantro

Line a plate with paper towels. In a large skillet, heat the oil over medium-high heat. Add the okra and cook until lightly browned, about 4 minutes. Transfer with a slotted spoon to the prepared plate.

Add the onion to the remaining oil in the skillet and cook, stirring occasionally, until golden, about 10 minutes. Add the garlic and ginger and cook until fragrant, 45–60 seconds. Add the cumin, coriander, cayenne pepper, and turmeric and stir to combine. Add the tomatoes with juices and stir to combine.

Cook until slightly thickened, about 5 minutes. Add the okra and stir to combine. Decrease the heat to medium-low and cook until the okra is tender, about 10 minutes. Taste and adjust for seasoning with salt and pepper. Garnish with the cilantro and serve immediately.

Okra Gougères

I wanted to incorporate okra into a fritter that wasn't fried, which, of course, is the antithesis of a fritter. Then I came up with the idea of baking beignet dough as the French do with their classic cheese puffs. I do believe this combination is about as "Bon appétit, y'all" as you can get!

MAKES 20 MEDIUM PUFFS

$3/4$ cup water

5 tablespoons unsalted butter

$1/2$ teaspoon coarse kosher salt

$1/2$ teaspoon crushed red pepper flakes, or to taste

1 teaspoon garlic powder

$3/4$ cup all-purpose flour

4 large eggs, at room temperature

4 ounces okra, stem ends trimmed, very thinly sliced

$3/4$ cup coarsely grated Gruyère

Preheat the oven to 375°. Line two baking sheets with silicone liners or parchment paper.

In a small saucepan, heat the water, butter, salt, red pepper flakes, and garlic powder until the butter is melted, then bring everything to a boil. Immediately remove the pan from the heat, add the flour all at once, and beat vigorously with a wooden spoon until the mixture is smooth and pulls away from the sides of the pan to form a ball, 30–60 seconds. Beat the mixture over low heat for 30–60 seconds more.

Remove the pan from the heat and, with a wooden spoon, beat the eggs into the dough one by one, beating thoroughly after each addition. Beat until the dough is shiny and just falls from the spoon.

Beat in the okra and grated cheese. Spoon 12 mounds about 2 inches in diameter onto each prepared baking sheet.

Place the baking sheets in the oven and bake until the dough is puffed and golden, rotating the baking sheets from top to bottom after 15 minutes, for a total of 25–30 minutes. To test for doneness, remove a puff from the baking sheet and let it cool for a minute. If it remains crisp on the outside, it's done. If it doesn't, replace it and continue cooking for 5 minutes longer. Remove the baking sheets to racks. Let the puffs cool slightly, then remove them from the baking sheets. Serve warm.

Pimento Cheese, Tomato, and Okra Cornmeal Cake Sandwiches

This recipe is summer on a plate. Instead of topping the okra cornmeal cakes with pimento cheese, try soft goat cheese, sheep's milk ricotta, or whipped herb cream cheese. Tasty additions to this new southern sandwich include bacon, avocado, microgreens, or broccoli sprouts.

MAKES 6 (3 ½-INCH) SANDWICHES

2 cups fine cornmeal (not self-rising)

2 teaspoons baking powder

1 teaspoon fine sea salt, or to taste

1 large egg, lightly beaten

1½ cups water, plus more if needed

8 ounces okra, stem ends trimmed, cut into ¼-inch pieces

1 jalapeño pepper, seeded and finely chopped

1 garlic clove, mashed into a paste

¼ cup canola oil, divided

Coarse kosher salt and freshly ground black pepper

6 tablespoons pimento cheese, plus more if needed

3 large tomatoes, thickly sliced

12 large basil leaves

6 leaves butterleaf, Boston, or Bibb lettuce

Line a baking sheet with paper towels. To prepare the batter, in a large bowl, whisk together the cornmeal, baking powder, and sea salt. In a second bowl or large liquid measuring cup, combine the egg and water. Add to the dry ingredients and whisk until smooth. Add the okra, jalapeño, and garlic. Stir to combine. (The batter should be thick but not dry. Add water as needed; the amount will depend on the size grind of the cornmeal. It will also thicken up a bit as it sits.)

To fry the cornmeal cakes, heat ⅛ cup of the oil in a cast-iron skillet over medium heat. Place ¼ cup batter in the heated skillet and smooth into an even layer. Repeat with additional batter, without crowding. Cook until the bottoms are brown and bubbles form on the tops and edges, 2–3 minutes. Turn and brown the other side, an additional 2–3 minutes. Transfer to the prepared baking sheet. While hot, season the cakes with salt and pepper. Repeat with the remaining batter and oil until you have 12 cornmeal cakes.

Place the cornmeal cakes on a clean work surface. Over 6 cakes, spread 1 tablespoon each pimento cheese. Top each with a slice of tomato and season with salt and pepper. Place 2 basil leaves and 1 lettuce leaf on each cake, then top with one of the remaining 6 cornmeal cakes. Enjoy immediately.

Okra Rice Cakes

These cakes were inspired by food stylist and friend Gloria Smiley and are a perfect use for leftover rice. If you have leftover rice, simply skip the rice-making process and start with ½ cup cooked rice. These cakes are an excellent base for grilled or steamed shrimp.

MAKES 4 RICE CAKES

1 quart water

¼ cup long-grain rice, preferably jasmine

½ teaspoon coarse kosher salt

4 tablespoons canola oil, plus more if needed, divided

1 shallot, finely chopped

1 garlic clove, very finely chopped

¼ pound okra, stem ends trimmed, cut into ¼-inch pieces

3 tablespoons all-purpose flour

1 tablespoon sesame seeds, preferably black

1 jalapeño pepper, seeded and chopped

2 large eggs, lightly beaten

¼ teaspoon cayenne pepper, or to taste

Coarse kosher salt and freshly ground black pepper

Bring the water to a boil in a small saucepan over high heat. Add the rice and salt. Bring to a boil, reduce the heat to simmer, and cover. Cook until tender, about 17 minutes. Drain well in a fine mesh sieve.

Meanwhile, line a baking sheet with paper towels. Heat 1 tablespoon of the oil in a large nonstick skillet over medium heat. Add the shallot and cook until soft and translucent, 3–5 minutes. Add the garlic and cook until fragrant, 45–60 seconds. Transfer to a large bowl. Wipe out the skillet with paper towels.

To the onion-garlic mixture, add the okra, cooked rice, flour, sesame seeds, jalapeño, eggs, and cayenne pepper. Season the mixture heartily with salt and pepper. Stir to combine.

To fry the cakes, heat the remaining 3 tablespoons oil over medium-high heat until shimmering. Using a large ice cream scoop or a ¼ cup measure, place a scoop of batter in the heated skillet and press into an even layer. Repeat with additional batter, without crowding. Cook the cakes until the bottoms are brown, 2–3 minutes. Turn and brown the other side, an additional 2–3 minutes. Transfer to the prepared plate. While hot, season the cakes with salt and pepper. Serve immediately.

Corn and Okra Pudding

Corn and okra make a happy marriage, further proof that what grows together, goes together. I've adapted this recipe from The Lee Bros. Southern Cookbook. *It's not a traditional southern recipe, but it's so good it makes you want to ask, "Why not?"*

MAKES 4–6 SERVINGS

1 tablespoon corn oil

¾ pound okra, stem ends trimmed, cut into ½-inch pieces

1½ cups lowfat milk

1 tablespoon fine cornmeal (not self-rising)

¼ teaspoon cayenne pepper, or to taste

1 teaspoon coarse kosher salt

Freshly ground white pepper

2 large eggs

2 cups sweet corn kernels (from about 4 ears corn)

2 tablespoons snipped chives

Preheat the oven to 350°. Grease a 2-quart baking dish with the oil.

Heat a large nonstick skillet over medium-high heat. Add the okra to the dry skillet and cook, stirring occasionally, until lightly browned, 8–10 minutes.

Meanwhile, heat the milk, cornmeal, and cayenne pepper in a small saucepan over medium heat until the milk just begins to simmer around the edges. Season with the salt and white pepper to taste.

In a large bowl, beat the eggs with a whisk until pale yellow. Slowly pour the milk mixture into the eggs, whisking constantly until smooth. Add the okra, corn, and chives. Transfer to the prepared baking dish. Bake until set and light golden brown, about 40 minutes. Serve immediately.

Okra Cornbread

I could make a whole meal out of buttered cornbread. The addition of vegetables renders this buttermilk cornbread absolutely divine. Except perhaps for fried chicken, cornbread is as close to religion in the South as any food gets. At the top of the list of cornbread sins is adding sugar. You'll notice a complete lack of sugar in this cornbread recipe. Sugar is more often found in what is referred to scathingly as "Yankee cornbread."

MAKES 6–8 SERVINGS

2 tablespoons unsalted butter or corn oil

2 cups medium-grind cornmeal (not self-rising)

1 teaspoon fine sea salt

1 teaspoon baking soda

¼ pound okra, stem ends trimmed, very thinly sliced

1 cup sweet corn kernels (from about 2 ears corn)

½ poblano pepper, seeded and chopped

1 onion, finely chopped

2 cups buttermilk

1 large egg, lightly beaten

Preheat the oven to 450°. Place the butter in a 9-inch cast-iron skillet or baking dish and heat in the oven for 10–15 minutes.

Meanwhile, in a bowl, combine the cornmeal, salt, and baking soda. Add the okra, corn, poblano pepper, and onion and toss to coat. In a large measuring cup, combine the buttermilk and egg. Add the wet ingredients to the dry and stir to combine.

Remove the heated skillet from the oven and pour the melted butter into the batter. Stir to combine, then pour the batter into the hot skillet. Bake until golden brown, about 35 minutes. Remove to a rack to cool slightly. Slice into wedges and serve warm.

Global Okra Recipes

In the global kitchen, I follow the path of okra around the world. We start our okra journey in Africa, the land of its birth. The ingredients don't seem unfamiliar to the southern table, possibly only the combinations. In Africa we find black-eyed peas, collard greens, peanuts, and sweet potatoes all combined with okra. Next, we journey to the Mediterranean region, Egypt, and the countries of Greece, Turkey, Morocco, and Iran. We then travel to India, a large country with many regions and styles of cuisine. There, okra, known as *bhindi*, is a very popular vegetable. In India's south, it's often prepared with coconut milk, while in the north, it's commonly prepared with onions and potatoes. Throughout the country, the dishes are prepared with warm to fiery hot spices. The Indian okra recipes absolutely burst with flavor. According to the Indian Ministry of Environment and Forests, India is responsible for 70 percent of okra production in the world. It seems these folks know what they're doing with okra. We then make a brief stop in Malaysia for a quick stir-fry. Last, we travel to the Caribbean and South America, where we find recipes bright with acid and citrus flavors.

West African Chicken Stew
with Okra and Peanuts
Màfe Ginaar

The cuisine of Senegal, which is situated on the western coast of Africa, is flavored with culinary influences from all over the world. The combination of chicken and peanuts is phenomenal and makes for a truly satisfying and tasty stew.

MAKES 4–6 SERVINGS

1 tablespoon canola oil

1½ pounds boneless, skinless chicken thighs, cut into
    1-inch pieces

Coarse kosher salt and freshly ground black pepper

1 onion, finely chopped

½ red bell pepper, seeded and chopped

3 garlic cloves, finely chopped

¼ cup tomato paste

½ cup crunchy peanut butter

1 habañero or Scotch bonnet pepper, seeded and finely chopped

1 bay leaf, preferably fresh

4 cups homemade chicken stock or reduced-fat, low-sodium
    chicken broth

3 carrots, halved lengthwise

10 okra pods, stem ends trimmed, halved lengthwise

2 sweet potatoes, peeled and cubed

½ small head green cabbage, quartered

Juice of 1 lime

Heat the oil in a large heavy-bottomed pot over medium-high heat until shimmering. Season the chicken with salt and pepper. Add the chicken to the pot and sear it, in two batches if necessary to avoid crowding, until brown on all sides. Transfer the chicken to a plate.

Add the onion and red bell pepper to the pot and cook, stirring, until the onion is soft and translucent, 3–5 minutes. Add the garlic and cook until fragrant, 45–60 seconds. Add the tomato paste and cook, stirring often, until lightly caramelized, about 2 minutes. Add the peanut butter, habañero, bay leaf, and stock. Stir until smooth, then add the chicken, carrots, okra, sweet potatoes, and cabbage and bring to a boil. Reduce the heat to medium-low and cook, covered partially and stirring occasionally, until the chicken is cooked and the vegetables are tender, about 25 minutes. Remove the bay leaf. Add the lime juice. Taste and adjust for seasoning with salt and pepper. Ladle into warmed bowls and serve immediately.

African Okra and Seafood Soup

This seafood soup is very likely the ancestor of gumbo. Fish sauce is packed with umami, the fifth taste after sour, salty, bitter, and sweet, and really makes the flavors pop in this fragrant and savory soup.

MAKES 6–8 SERVINGS

¼ cup palm or canola oil
2 onions, roughly chopped
4 garlic cloves, chopped
½-inch coin of ginger, peeled and finely chopped
1 habañero or Scotch bonnet pepper, seeded and chopped
12 cups seafood or vegetable stock
2 tablespoons dried shrimp
1 large eggplant, peeled and cut into large chunks
1 pound okra, stem ends trimmed, cut into ½-inch pieces
2 tomatoes, chopped
3 bay leaves, preferably fresh
24 mussels, cleaned and debearded
18 large (21/25 count) shrimp, peeled and deveined
1 pound thick white fish fillet, such as cod, halibut,
    or barramundi, cut into 1½-inch cubes
Coarse kosher salt and freshly ground black pepper
Cooked rice, for serving

Heat the oil in a large pot over medium-high heat until shimmering. Add the onions and cook until soft and translucent, 3–5 minutes. Add the garlic, ginger, and habañero and cook until fragrant, 45–60 seconds. (Be careful not to breathe in the steam because habañeros are very hot.) Add the stock, dried shrimp, eggplant, okra, tomato, and bay leaves. Cover and reduce the heat to medium-low and cook until the vegetables are quite tender, about 45 minutes.

Remove the bay leaves. In the pot, using an immersion blender, purée the soup until smooth. Or ladle the soup into a blender a little at a time and purée until smooth, then return it to the pot.

Add the mussels, shrimp, and fish to the puréed liquid. Stir to combine. Cover and cook until the seafood is cooked through, about 4 minutes. Season with salt and pepper. Spoon rice into warmed bowls, then ladle over the soup, making sure everyone has a bit of seafood. Serve immediately.

Congolese Okra and Greens

For southerners used to fatback or hog jowls in their greens, the peanut butter in this recipe will be a surprise. Here I'm substituting it for palm butter. Palm oil and palm butter are both derived from the fruit of a particular palm tree. Palm oil, used in African, Asian, and Brazilian cooking, is slightly easier to find.

MAKES 6 SERVINGS

---

1 tablespoon palm or canola oil

1 onion, chopped

1 cup homemade chicken stock or reduced-fat, low-sodium chicken broth

2 cups creamy peanut butter

1½ pounds collard greens, stems removed and chopped

¾ pound okra, stem ends trimmed

2 hot chili peppers, preferably red, such as bird's eye, chopped

Coarse kosher salt and freshly ground black pepper

Heat the oil in a large saucepan over medium-high heat. Add the onion and cook until soft and translucent, 3–5 minutes. Add the stock and peanut butter and stir until smooth. Add the collard greens, okra, and chili peppers. Season with salt and pepper. Reduce the heat to simmer and cook until the vegetables are tender, about 20 minutes. Taste and adjust for seasoning with salt and pepper. Serve immediately.

Nigerian Black-Eyed Pea and Okra Fritters

Akara Awon

The seemingly unorthodox method of preparing the black-eyes for the fritter batter in this recipe showcases the technique of making bean, not wheat, flour. Traditionally, the skins of the peas are removed, but I've omitted that step since it's a bit troublesome and the fritters are tasty with the skins on, too.

MAKES ABOUT 35 FRITTERS

1 cup dried black-eyed peas
1½ cups water, divided
4 okra pods, stem ends trimmed, very finely chopped
½ onion, finely chopped
1 habañero or Scotch bonnet pepper, seeded and finely chopped
¼-inch coin of ginger, peeled and minced
Coarse kosher salt and freshly ground black pepper
4 cups peanut oil

Place the peas in a large bowl and cover with 1 cup of the water. Soak overnight, then drain. Place the peas in the bowl of a food processor fitted with a blade. Pulse until smooth. Transfer the paste to a large bowl. Add the remaining ½ cup water, okra, onion, habañero, and ginger. Season heartily with salt and pepper. Stir to combine.

Line a plate with paper towels and set by the cooktop. Heat the oil in a medium heavy-duty pot over medium-high heat. To fry the fritters, using a small ice cream scoop, carefully drop the dough into the hot oil without crowding. Fry, stirring occasionally with a slotted spoon, until the fritters are golden brown, 3–5 minutes. Remove with a slotted spoon to the prepared plate. Adjust the heat to maintain the proper temperature and repeat with the remaining batter. Season with salt. Serve immediately.

Egyptian Okra and Chickpeas

Chickpeas are packed with vitamins, nutrients, and a rich, almost meaty flavor. Canned chickpeas are very handy to have in the pantry, but if you have the time, cooking dried chickpeas from scratch adds a whole new level to this dish that blends nicely with the okra and tomatoes. One cup of dried chickpeas makes 2½ cups of cooked chickpeas; 1 (15½-ounce) can of chickpeas contains 2 heaping cups. The yields aren't exactly the same, but they're close enough to be interchangeable.

MAKES 4–6 SERVINGS

- 1 cup dried chickpeas, soaked overnight, or 1 (15½-ounce) can chickpeas
- 2 tablespoons extra-virgin olive oil
- 2 garlic cloves, very finely chopped
- 1 pound okra, stem ends trimmed
- 1 (14½-ounce) can diced tomatoes with juices
- 1 tablespoon ground cumin
- Coarse kosher salt and freshly ground black pepper
- Zest and juice of 1 lemon
- ½ cup coarsely chopped flat-leaf parsley
- Warm pita bread and olive oil, for dipping

If using dried chickpeas, place the soaked chickpeas in a medium saucepan, cover with water, and bring to a boil over medium-high heat. Add 1 teaspoon of salt. Reduce the heat to medium-low and gently simmer until the chickpeas are just tender, about 20 minutes. Remove from the heat. Remove 1 cup of the chickpea cooking liquid and reserve. Leave the cooked chickpeas in the remaining liquid to keep them moist.

Meanwhile, heat the olive oil in a large, deep skillet over medium-low heat. Add the garlic and cook, stirring occasionally, until fragrant, 45–60 seconds. Add the okra and cook, stirring once or twice, until it turns bright green, about 3 minutes.

Add the tomatoes with juices, reserved chickpea liquid, and cumin. (If using canned chickpeas, substitute 1 cup water or chicken stock for the chickpea cooking liquid. Do not use the liquid from the can as it often tastes metallic.) Season with salt and pepper. Cover, reduce the heat to low, and cook until the okra is tender, about 20 minutes.

Drain the chickpeas, discarding any remaining cooking liquid. If using canned chickpeas, drain and rinse them. Add the chickpeas to the okra mixture and stir to combine. Cover and cook just until the chickpeas are heated through, about 5 minutes. Add the lemon zest, lemon juice, and parsley. Stir to combine. Taste and adjust for seasoning with salt and pepper. Serve hot, warm, or at room temperature with pita bread and olive oil, for dipping.

Moroccan Lamb and Okra Tagine with Preserved Lemons

Lamb is earthy and rich, but the fat can be overwhelming and strong, especially when chilled or at room temperature. Remove as much fat as possible before cooking. Goat and lamb are the most common meats eaten in the Middle East. The preserved lemons take 3–4 weeks to cure. You may substitute commercially prepared preserved lemons, available at Middle Eastern markets.

MAKES 4–6 SERVINGS

FOR THE PRESERVED LEMONS (MAKES 1 QUART)
8 lemons, well scrubbed
3 cups coarse kosher salt
Fresh lemon juice, as needed

FOR THE TAGINE
$\frac{1}{4}$ cup hot water
$\frac{1}{4}$ teaspoon saffron threads
2 tablespoons olive oil
$1\frac{1}{2}$ pounds lamb shoulder, cut into 2-inch pieces
Coarse kosher salt and freshly ground black pepper
1 onion, chopped
3 garlic cloves, finely chopped
1 teaspoon ras el hanout
3 cups homemade chicken stock or reduced-fat, low-sodium chicken broth
2 cinnamon sticks
1 pound okra, stem ends trimmed, cut into $\frac{1}{2}$-inch pieces
1 cup English peas
2 tablespoons chopped flat-leaf parsley
2 tablespoons chopped cilantro
1–2 preserved lemons, chopped, and flatbread, for serving

To make the preserved lemons, cut the tips off the ends of the lemons. Stopping just short of the stem end, cut each lemon into quarters lengthwise, being careful to leave them attached. Pack the cavities of the lemons with as much salt as they will hold.

Place the lemons in a sterilized wide-mouth quart-size jar, packing them in as tightly as possible. As you push the lemons into the jar, some juice will be squeezed out of them. When the jar is full, the juice should cover the lemons; if it doesn't, add some freshly squeezed lemon juice.

Seal the jar and set it aside for 3–4 weeks until the lemon rinds become soft, turning and gently shaking the jar daily to keep the salt well distributed. The lemons should be covered with juice at all times; add more juice if needed. Rinse the lemons before using.

To make the tagine, combine the water and saffron. Line a plate with paper towels. Heat the olive oil in a large heavy-bottomed pot over medium-high heat until shimmering. Season the lamb with salt and pepper. Sear the lamb in 2–3 batches without crowding until nicely browned on all sides. Remove to the prepared plate.

Once all of the lamb has been seared, add the onion and cook until soft and translucent, 3–5 minutes. Add the garlic and cook until fragrant, 45–60 seconds. Add the ras el hanout and stir to combine. Add the saffron and water, stock, and cinnamon. Return the lamb to the pot and stir to combine. Cover and bring to a boil over high heat. Reduce the heat to simmer. Cook, covered, stirring occasionally, until the lamb is mostly tender, about 45 minutes.

Add the okra and peas and cook until the lamb and vegetables are tender, about 20 minutes. Add the parsley and cilantro and stir to combine. Taste and adjust for seasoning with salt and pepper. Ladle into warmed serving bowls and serve with the preserved lemons and flatbread.

Iranian Okra Khoresh
Khoresh Bamieh

Khoresh *generally refers to different stews served with rice in Persian cuisine. Many okra dishes are served with rice. Rice is thought to have originated in Asia, but studies suggest that African slaves who spread okra throughout the world also helped spread the cultivation of rice.*

MAKES 6 SERVINGS

4 tablespoons canola oil, plus more if needed, divided

1 eggplant, peeled and cubed

1 pound lamb, goat, or beef, cut into 1-inch cubes

Coarse kosher salt and freshly ground pepper

2 onions, sliced

2 garlic cloves, very finely chopped

2 cups water

3 tablespoons tomato paste

1 teaspoon ground turmeric

Juice of 1 lime

1 pound okra, stem ends trimmed, cut into ½-inch pieces

Cooked rice, for serving

Line a plate with paper towels. Heat 2 tablespoons of the oil in a large heavy-bottomed pot over medium-high heat until shimmering. Add the eggplant and fry until golden brown on all sides. Remove to the prepared plate.

Heat the remaining oil in the same pot. Season the lamb with salt and pepper. Sear the lamb in 2–3 batches without crowding until nicely browned on all sides. Remove to the plate with the eggplant.

Once all of the lamb has been seared, add the onions. Cook until golden brown, 5 minutes. Add the garlic and cook until fragrant, 45–60 seconds. Add the water, tomato paste, and turmeric. Return the lamb and eggplant to the pot and stir to combine. Cover and bring to a boil over high heat. Reduce the heat to simmer. Cook, covered, stirring occasionally, until the lamb is mostly tender, about 45 minutes.

When the meat is tender, add the lime juice and okra. Simmer, uncovered, until just tender, about 20 minutes. Taste and adjust for seasoning with salt and pepper. Serve immediately over rice.

Turkish Okra and Ground Beef
Kiymali Bamya

There's as much okra as meat in this dish, which is not quite a stew and not quite a sauce. Kiymali *translates as "minced meat" in Turkish.*

MAKES 4–6 SERVINGS

---

1 pound okra, stem ends trimmed, cut into ¼-inch pieces
Juice of 1 lemon
2 tablespoons olive oil
1 onion, sliced
2 garlic cloves, very finely chopped
1 teaspoon ground cumin
1 teaspoon ground coriander
1 pound lean ground beef
Coarse kosher salt and freshly ground black pepper
¾ cup hot water
2 tablespoons tomato paste
2 tablespoons chopped mint
Cooked rice or bulgur, for serving

Place the okra in a bowl and add the lemon juice. Set aside at room temperature to marinate, about 15 minutes.

Heat the olive oil in a heavy-bottomed pan over medium heat. Add the onion and cook until soft and translucent, 3–5 minutes. Add the garlic and cook until fragrant, 45–60 seconds. Add the cumin, coriander, and ground beef, breaking up any big clumps. Season with salt and pepper. Cook, stirring occasionally, about 5 minutes. Add the water, tomato paste, and mint. Stir to combine.

Add the okra and lemon juice. Cover and bring to a boil over high heat. Reduce the heat to simmer. Cook until the okra is tender, about 20 minutes. Taste and adjust for seasoning with salt and pepper. Serve immediately over rice.

Crisp Greek Fried Okra
Bamyies Tiganites

While researching recipes for this book, I quickly realized that every culture that utilizes okra in its cuisine has a fried okra recipe. This Greek recipe would be at home in the Deep South, India, or Africa. It's important to fry only ½ cup or so of okra at a time to keep the oil piping hot. Also, this recipe calls for plain olive oil, not extra-virgin, because it has a higher smoke point and is better for frying.

MAKES 4–6 SERVINGS

1½ cups olive oil
1 pound okra, stem ends trimmed, very thinly sliced
Fine sea salt
½ teaspoon cayenne pepper, or to taste

Line a baking sheet with paper towels. Heat the olive oil in a large cast-iron skillet over medium heat until it reaches 350° on a deep-fat thermometer. When the oil is hot, add about ½ cup of the okra. Stir with a slotted spoon to turn the okra in the oil. Cook until crisp and brown, 2–2½ minutes. Remove with the slotted spoon to the prepared baking sheet. Sprinkle with sea salt and the cayenne pepper. Repeat with the remaining okra. Serve immediately.

Greek Okra Ragout
Bamyies Yiahni

Greeks call okra by its Arabic name, bamya, *or* bamyies *in the plural. Greek cooks often soak okra in vinegar before cooking to keep it crisp.*

MAKES 4–6 SERVINGS

1 pound okra, stem ends trimmed
1 cup red wine vinegar, divided
¼ cup olive oil
2 onions, sliced
3 garlic cloves, finely chopped
2 plum tomatoes, peeled and coarsely chopped
    (see Cooking Tip, page 43)
1 cup water, plus more if needed
Coarse kosher salt and freshly ground black pepper
¼ cup chopped flat-leaf parsley
4 ounces feta cheese (optional)

Place the okra in a glass or stainless steel bowl. Remove 1 tablespoon of red wine vinegar from the cup and reserve. Pour the remaining vinegar over the okra and stir to coat. Set aside at room temperature, stirring occasionally, for 30 minutes. Drain and rinse the okra thoroughly in a colander under cold running water. Shake well to remove excess water.

Heat the olive oil in a large heavy-bottomed pot over medium-high heat. Add the onions and cook until soft and translucent, 3–5 minutes. Add the garlic and cook until fragrant, 45–60 seconds. Add the okra, stir to combine, and reduce the heat to simmer. Add the tomatoes and water. Season with salt and pepper.

Bring to a boil, then reduce the heat to simmer. Cover and simmer, stirring occasionally, over low heat for about 45 minutes, or until the okra is very tender. Add the parsley and remaining tablespoon of red wine vinegar. Taste and adjust for seasoning with salt and pepper. (Be careful not to add too much salt if serving with feta as the cheese can be quite salty.) Transfer to small serving plates and serve with slices of feta, if desired, or transfer to a serving bowl and top with crumbled feta. Serve immediately.

Greek Stewed Okra
with Green Beans and Bulgur

Bulgur, a nutritious staple in the Mediterranean, is wheat kernels that have been steamed, dried, and then crushed. It's often used in tabbouleh and sometimes is mistakenly confused with cracked wheat. In this dish, okra and green beans make a lovely couple.

MAKES 4–6 SERVINGS

1 pound okra, stem ends trimmed

¼ cup white wine vinegar

½ pound green beans, stem ends and strings removed

¼ cup olive oil

2 onions, chopped

1 (14½-ounce) can whole tomatoes with juices

¾ cup chopped flat-leaf parsley

½ teaspoon crushed red pepper flakes, or to taste

Coarse kosher salt and freshly ground black pepper

½ cup quick-cooking bulgur

¾ cups homemade chicken stock or reduced-fat, low-sodium chicken broth

Place the okra in a glass or stainless steel bowl. Pour the vinegar over it and stir to coat. Set aside at room temperature, stirring occasionally, for 30 minutes. Drain and rinse the okra thoroughly in a colander under cold running water. Shake well to remove excess water.

Meanwhile, make an ice-water bath by filling a large bowl with ice and water. Line a plate with paper towels. To cook the green beans, bring a large pot of salted water to a rolling boil over high heat. Add the beans and cook until crisp-tender, about 3 minutes. Drain well in a colander, then set the colander with the beans in the ice-water bath (to set the color and stop the cooking), making sure the beans are submerged. Once cooled, remove the beans to the prepared plate.

Heat the olive oil in a large, shallow, stainless steel skillet with a lid over medium-high heat. Add the onions and cook until soft and translucent, 3–5 minutes. Add the okra, green beans, tomatoes with juices, parsley, and red pepper flakes. Season with salt and pepper. Reduce the heat to low, cover, and simmer until the beans and okra are tender, about 10 minutes.

Add the bulgur and stock; stir to combine. Simmer on low for another 20 minutes. Remove from the heat and set aside, covered, for 5 minutes, until the bulgur has absorbed the liquid. Taste and adjust for seasoning with salt and pepper. Serve immediately.

Indian Fried Okra with Spiced Yogurt
Bhindi Raita

Traditionally, the okra in this recipe is sliced, fried, and stirred into the spicy yogurt sauce. I think it makes an excellent finger-food appetizer fried whole with the sauce served on the side. Chickpea flour, also called garbanzo flour, can be found online or in Indian markets. You may also use Bob's Red Mill Garbanzo & Fava Bean Flour, found at health food stores or in the gluten-free section of better grocery stores.

MAKES 4–6 SERVINGS

1½ tablespoons chickpea flour

½ tablespoon cumin seeds, crushed

1 cup plain 2% Greek-style yogurt

1 teaspoon chopped cilantro

Coarse kosher salt and freshly ground black pepper

½ cup canola oil

1 pound okra, stem ends trimmed

1 teaspoon curry powder, preferably Madras

¼ teaspoon cayenne pepper, or to taste

½ tablespoon ground coriander

To make the dipping sauce, place the chickpea flour and cumin seeds in a small dry skillet over moderate heat. Cook, stirring constantly to prevent scorching, until toasted, 2–3 minutes. Transfer to a bowl. Add the yogurt and cilantro; season with salt and pepper. Stir until smooth.

Line a large bowl with paper towels. Heat the oil in a large skillet over medium-high heat until shimmering. Add the okra and fry, stirring often, until crisp and browned, about 15 minutes. Remove with a slotted spoon to the prepared bowl. Toss to dry, then remove the paper towels, leaving the okra in the bowl. While the okra is still hot, sprinkle it with the curry powder, cayenne pepper, and coriander. Season with salt and pepper and toss to coat. Set aside and keep warm. To serve, place the warm spiced okra on a platter with the dipping sauce at the center.

Indian Chicken and Okra Curry
Murgh Bhindi Kari

Chicken thighs are best for curries and stews because the meat doesn't dry out and become stringy and tough. If you want to use boneless, skinless chicken breasts for a slightly lighter version, check the chicken toward the shorter end of the cooking time.

MAKES 4–6 SERVINGS

1½ pounds boneless, skinless chicken thighs

Coarse kosher salt and freshly ground black pepper

2 tablespoons canola oil

1 onion, chopped

3 garlic cloves, finely chopped

2 teaspoons curry powder, preferably Madras

¼ teaspoon cayenne pepper, or to taste

1 (13½-ounce) can lowfat coconut milk

1 (14½-ounce) can diced tomatoes with juices

¼ cup golden raisins

1 pound okra, stem ends trimmed

Cooked rice, for serving

2 tablespoons coarsely chopped cilantro

Season the chicken with salt and pepper. Heat the oil in a large skillet over medium-high heat until shimmering. Add the chicken and cook, turning once, until brown, about 5 minutes total. (The chicken will still be raw but will cook further in the sauce.) Transfer the chicken to a plate.

Reduce the heat to medium. Add the onion to the skillet and cook until soft and translucent, 3–5 minutes. Add the garlic and cook until fragrant, 45–60 seconds. Add the curry powder, cayenne pepper, coconut milk, tomatoes with juices, and raisins; stir to combine. Add the okra and chicken along with any juices accumulated on the plate. Simmer, stirring occasionally, until the chicken is cooked through and the okra is tender, 15–20 minutes. Taste and adjust for seasoning with salt and pepper. Spoon rice into warmed bowls. Ladle over the curry and top with the cilantro. Serve immediately.

Indian Okra and Potatoes in Green Masala

Seyala Bhindyoon Patata

Masala *is simply a number of spices and other ingredients ground into a paste or powder for use in Indian cooking. This hearty vegetarian side dish is excellent served with grilled or even store-bought rotisserie chicken.*

MAKES 4–6 SERVINGS

1 small bunch cilantro, leaves and tender stems only
1 onion, roughly chopped
1 serrano chili pepper, stem removed and coarsely chopped
1/4-inch coin of ginger, peeled and coarsely chopped
4 garlic cloves
1 tablespoon canola oil
1 tomato, seeded and finely chopped
1 teaspoon ground coriander
1/4 teaspoon cayenne pepper, or to taste
1/4 teaspoon ground turmeric
1 1/2 cups water, plus more if needed
1 pound okra, stem ends trimmed
3 medium Yukon Gold potatoes, peeled and sliced 1/4 inch thick
Coarse kosher salt and freshly ground black pepper

Combine the cilantro, onion, chili pepper, ginger, and garlic in the bowl of a food processor fitted with a blade. Purée until smooth. Heat the oil in a medium skillet over medium heat. Add the cilantro purée. Cook, stirring, until slightly thickened, about 5 minutes.

Add the tomato, coriander, cayenne pepper, turmeric, and water. Cover and cook over low heat until the sauce has thickened and blended, about 10 minutes.

Add the okra and potatoes and stir to combine. Bring to a boil, then reduce the heat to simmer. Season with salt and pepper. Cover and simmer until the vegetables are tender, about 20 minutes. Taste and adjust for seasoning with salt and pepper. Serve immediately.

Indian Spiced Okra in Yogurt Gravy
Vendaka Masala Pachdi

Since this recipe calls for half a can of coconut milk, I suggest that you place the unused half in an airtight container and freeze it instead of letting it languish and spoil in your refrigerator. Curry leaves may be found at Indian markets and add a smoky, earthy component to this flavorful stew. Serve with roasted potatoes for a filling vegetarian dinner.

MAKES 6 SERVINGS

---

2 tablespoons canola oil

1 teaspoon yellow mustard seeds

1 teaspoon cumin seeds

$\frac{1}{2}$ teaspoon crushed red pepper flakes, or to taste

2 tablespoons black lentils, or *urid daal*

2 onions, chopped

2 tomatoes, seeded and chopped

3 teaspoons ground coriander

1 teaspoon ground turmeric

1 teaspoon paprika

$\frac{1}{2}$ teaspoon cayenne pepper, or to taste

2 pounds okra, stem ends trimmed

$\frac{1}{2}$ (13$\frac{1}{2}$-ounce) can lowfat coconut milk

$\frac{3}{4}$ cup plain 2% Greek-style yogurt

$\frac{1}{2}$ cup cashews, chopped

10–12 curry leaves (optional)

Coarse kosher salt and freshly ground black pepper

Heat the oil in a medium saucepan over medium-high heat. Add the mustard seeds, cumin seeds, red pepper flakes, and lentils. Cook until the spices are fragrant and start to pop, about 30–45 seconds. (I found my oil splatter screen to be quite helpful!)

Add the onions and cook until soft and translucent, 3–5 minutes. Add the tomatoes, coriander, turmeric, paprika, cayenne pepper, and okra. Cook, stirring occasionally, until the tomatoes become soft, about 5 minutes. Add the coconut milk, yogurt, cashews, and curry leaves, if desired. Stir to combine. Cook until the okra is tender, an additional 10 minutes. Season with salt and pepper. Serve immediately.

Indian Spicy Sweet Okra with Peanuts
Bhindi Nu Shaak

The double dose of cumin is a one-two punch of delicious flavor. The touch of brown sugar in this spicy side dish is surprising, and the hint of caramel rounds out the warm spices. The freshness of the cilantro added at the end helps the flavors pop. If you're not a big fan of cilantro, try flat-leaf parsley instead.

MAKES 4–6 SERVINGS

1 tablespoon peanut oil
1 teaspoon cumin seeds
1 pound okra, stem ends trimmed
¼ cup dry-roasted, unsalted peanuts, chopped
1 tablespoon brown sugar, or to taste
1 teaspoon ground cumin
¼ teaspoon crushed red pepper flakes, or to taste
Coarse kosher salt and freshly ground black pepper
¼ cup chopped cilantro

Heat the oil in a large skillet over medium heat. Add the cumin seeds and cook until fragrant, 10–15 seconds. Add the okra, peanuts, brown sugar, cumin, and red pepper flakes. Season with salt and pepper; stir to combine. Cook over high heat until the okra is bright green, 2–3 minutes. Reduce the heat to low. Cover and simmer, stirring occasionally, until the okra is tender, about 15 minutes. Add the cilantro and stir to combine. Taste and adjust for seasoning with salt and pepper. Serve immediately.

Singapore-Style Sambal Oelek Okra

Sambal oelek *is a chili sauce of Indonesian and Malaysian origin. It's made from a variety of different chilies and is most often used in cooking, not as a condiment like* sriracha. *This dish has a heavy dose of umami with the use of dried shrimp. It will light up your mouth with flavor!*

MAKES 4–6 SERVINGS

¼ cup canola oil
1 large shallot, chopped
2 tablespoons sambal oelek
1 tablespoon dried shrimp, very finely chopped
2 garlic cloves, very finely chopped
¼-inch coin of ginger, peeled and finely chopped
¾ pound okra, stem ends trimmed, cut diagonally into
    ¼-inch pieces
Coarse kosher salt and freshly ground black pepper

Line a plate with paper towels. Heat the oil in a large skillet over medium-high heat until very hot, almost smoking. When the oil is hot, add the shallot to the skillet. Cook until browned and crisp, about 2 minutes. Using a slotted spoon, transfer the shallot to the prepared plate, making sure to get every last bit. In a small bowl, add the sambal oelek, shrimp, garlic, and ginger. Stir to combine and set aside.

Reheat the oil until very hot. Add the okra to the hot oil and fry until bright green, about 2 minutes. Add the sambal oelek mixture and shallot. Stir-fry over high heat until combined, about 1 minute. Season with salt, but not too much as the dried shrimp are quite salty. Transfer the okra to a warmed shallow serving bowl. Taste and adjust for seasoning with salt and pepper. Serve immediately.

Cuban Pork with Yellow Rice, Okra, and Annatto Oil

Cerdo con Arroz Amarillo Qimbombo

Undoubtedly, okra is part of the cuisine and food culture of any place that was involved in the slave trade. Throughout the Caribbean and further south into Central and South America, there are vestiges of African cooking. This dish was originally prepared with less-expensive cuts of meat, but for the modern kitchen, I've adapted the recipe to include leaner, quicker-cooking pork loin.

Annatto seeds, also known as achiote seeds, are used throughout Latin America to add a distinctive red color to sautéed foods, especially chicken and seafood, as well as to rice pilaf. They're available at Latin American markets and in the Latin American section of many supermarkets.

MAKES 6 SERVINGS

FOR THE ANNATTO OIL (MAKES 1 CUP)
¼ cup annatto seeds
1 cup pure olive oil

FOR THE PORK
2 pounds pork loin, cut into ½-inch cubes
Juice of 1 orange
Juice of 1 lime
5 garlic cloves, very finely chopped
1 teaspoon ground cumin
Coarse kosher salt and freshly ground black pepper
1 onion, chopped
1 red bell pepper, seeded and chopped
2 garlic cloves, very finely chopped
1½ cups long-grain rice
2 tomatoes, seeded and diced

¼ pound okra, stem ends trimmed, cut into ½-inch pieces

3 cups homemade chicken stock or reduced-fat, low-sodium
chicken broth

1 thyme sprig

1 cilantro sprig, plus ¼ cup chopped cilantro

To make the annatto oil, combine the annatto seeds and olive oil in a small saucepan over medium heat. Bring to just a simmer, moderating the heat so the oil never boils. Cook until the oil is bright red, about 20 minutes. Strain through a fine mesh sieve and discard the seeds. Store the oil in an airtight container in the refrigerator for up to 4 weeks.

To make the pork, in a medium bowl, combine the pork, orange juice, lime juice, garlic, and cumin. Season heartily with salt and pepper. Cover and refrigerate to marinate for at least 6 hours or overnight.

Heat 3 tablespoons annatto oil in a large pot over medium-high heat until shimmering. Add the pork to the oil and sear, without crowding, on all sides until lightly browned, about 5 minutes. Using a slotted spoon, remove the pork to a plate.

Add another 3 tablespoons annatto oil to the pot. Add the onion and red bell pepper and cook until the onion is golden brown, about 5 minutes. Add the garlic and cook until fragrant, 45–60 seconds. Add the rice and cook, stirring constantly to toast and set the color in the rice, about 2 minutes.

Add the tomatoes, okra, stock, thyme sprig, and cilantro sprig. Stir to combine. Cover and bring to a boil. Reduce the heat to simmer. Cook until the pork is cooked through and the rice and vegetables are tender, about 20 minutes. Remove from the heat and let rest for 5 minutes. Remove the thyme and cilantro sprigs. Taste and adjust for seasoning with salt and pepper. Transfer to a warmed serving bowl and garnish with the chopped cilantro. Serve immediately.

Jamaican Curried Shrimp and Okra

This dish tastes best when prepared with homemade seafood stock. Peel the shrimp, place the peels in a pot, and add just enough water to cover, at least 1½ cups. Add a few sprigs of parsley and thyme, a quartered onion, chopped carrot, and chopped celery and bring to a boil. Simmer until fragrant and flavorful, about 15 minutes, then strain. This simple step will make a world of difference in your finished dish.

MAKES 4–6 SERVINGS

1 tablespoon canola oil

2 tablespoons curry powder

1 onion, chopped

1 scallion, chopped (white and tender green parts)

¼ red bell pepper, seeded and diced

½ habañero or Scotch bonnet pepper, seeded and chopped

1 garlic clove, chopped

2 tablespoons tomato paste

1 cup seafood stock or water

½ pound okra, stem ends trimmed, cut into ¼-inch pieces

1 pound large shrimp (21/25 count), peeled and deveined

Coarse kosher salt and freshly ground black pepper

Cooked rice, for serving

Heat the oil in a large skillet over medium-low heat. Add the curry powder. Cook, stirring, until fragrant and toasted, about 2 minutes. Add the onion, scallion, red bell pepper, and habañero. (Be careful not to breathe in the steam because habañeros are very hot.) Cook until the onion is soft and translucent, about 3 minutes. Add the garlic and cook until fragrant, 45–60 seconds. Add the tomato paste and stock; stir to combine.

Increase the heat, then add the okra and cook until bright green, about 3 minutes. Add the shrimp and stir to combine. Season with salt and pepper. Reduce the heat to medium, cover, and cook until the shrimp are pink, about 5 minutes. Taste and adjust for seasoning with salt and pepper. Serve immediately over rice.

Jamaican Cornmeal-and-Okra Mush

Cornmeal mush is a common dish in Caribbean Creole cuisine. It's known as fungi *in Saint Croix and Antigua,* coo-coo *in the Bahamas, and* mayi moulin *in Haiti. The southern version of cornmeal mush is finely ground grits, since both are made of ground corn. Regardless of what you call the dish, it's traditionally served with, and positively delicious with, fried fish. Break out this version at your next fish fry.*

MAKES 4–6 SERVINGS

1 tablespoon canola oil

6 scallions, chopped (white and tender green parts)

1 tomato, seeded and chopped

¼ red bell pepper, seeded and chopped

½ pound okra, stem ends trimmed, cut into ¼-inch pieces

1 (13½-ounce) can lowfat coconut milk

¼ cup water, plus more if needed

1 cup fine cornmeal (not self-rising)

¼ habañero or Scotch bonnet pepper, seeded and chopped

½ teaspoon chopped thyme

Coarse kosher salt and freshly ground black pepper

Heat the oil in a medium saucepan over medium-high heat until shimmering. Add the scallions, tomato, red bell pepper, and okra. Cook, stirring often, until the vegetables are slightly tender, 3–5 minutes. Add the coconut milk and water and bring to a boil. Whisk in the cornmeal, habañero, and thyme; season with salt and pepper. Bring to a boil over high heat. Reduce the heat to simmer and cook, stirring frequently, until tender, about 20 minutes. (Depending on the grind of the cornmeal, you may need to add more water, but the mixture should be quite thick.) Taste and adjust for seasoning with salt and pepper. Serve immediately.

Haitian Beef with Okra and Pikliz Vinegar

Viand Bef Ak Kalalou

Pikliz vinegar is a traditional Haitian condiment, but it's really more of a slaw than a vinegar. It makes the flavors pop in this rustic stew. Steaming instead of stewing the meat is unorthodox, but it makes the flavors of the marinade penetrate the meat deeply, with delicious results.

MAKES 4–6 SERVINGS

FOR THE VINEGAR (MAKES ABOUT 2 1/2 CUPS)
1/4 small head green cabbage, cored and very thinly sliced
1 carrot, grated
1/2 red onion, very thinly sliced
1 tablespoon distilled white vinegar
1/2 habañero or Scotch bonnet pepper, seeded and chopped
Pinch of ground cloves
Coarse kosher salt and freshly ground black pepper

FOR THE BEEF
3 pounds beef chuck, cubed
1 lime, halved
1/2 red bell pepper, seeded and thinly sliced
1/2 green bell pepper, seeded and thinly sliced
1 onion, thinly sliced, divided
2 scallions, chopped (white and tender green parts)
3 garlic cloves, chopped
1/4 teaspoon ground cloves
2 tablespoons tomato paste
4 1/2 cups water, divided, plus more if needed
4 small carrots, sliced into 1/2-inch rounds

1 pound okra, stem ends trimmed
1 thyme sprig
Coarse kosher salt and freshly ground black pepper
Cooked rice, for serving

To make the pikliz vinegar, in a large bowl, combine the cabbage, carrot, red onion, vinegar, habañero, and cloves. Toss to coat. Season with salt and pepper. Store in an airtight container for up to 24 hours.

To make the beef, place the meat in a medium stainless steel or glass bowl. Rub with the halved lime, then squeeze over the juice. Discard the lime halves. Add ½ cup pikliz vinegar, the bell peppers, half of the onion, the scallions, the garlic, and the cloves. Cover and refrigerate, turning occasionally, for at least 2 hours or overnight.

Transfer the meat and marinating juices to a large, heavy-bottomed pot over medium heat. Cook, covered, checking occasionally, until the marinating liquid starts to evaporate, about 30 minutes. Combine the tomato paste and ½ cup of the water in a small bowl. Add to the pot and stir to combine. Continue cooking over medium heat, stirring occasionally, for an additional 20 minutes. (Add more water if the mixture starts to stick.)

Add the remaining half of the onion, carrots, okra, thyme sprig, and remaining 4 cups of water; stir to combine. Bring to a boil over high heat, then reduce the heat to simmer. Cover and cook, stirring occasionally, for an additional 20 minutes. Remove the thyme sprig. Taste and adjust for seasoning with salt and pepper. Serve over rice with additional pikliz vinegar on the side.

Callaloo and Crab Soup

Callaloo *is the name of a traditional West Indian soup from Trinidad and Tobago, as well as the large leafy greens, also known as* dasheen *or taro root leaves, that are its chief component. Spinach is a good substitute. Okra, known as* ochro, *is the other main ingredient in* callaloo. *Traditionally, raw crab is chopped whole in the shell and added, but for ease of service, I'm calling for seafood stock and picked crabmeat.*

MAKES 4–6 SERVINGS

1 teaspoon canola oil

1 onion, coarsely chopped

1 garlic clove, finely chopped

1 habañero or Scotch bonnet pepper, seeded and chopped

10 ounces spinach, stems trimmed, chopped

½ pound okra, stem ends trimmed, chopped

1 scallion, chopped (white and tender green parts)

2 thyme sprigs, leaves only

2 flat-leaf parsley sprigs, leaves only

4 cups seafood stock or water

Coarse kosher salt and freshly ground black pepper

1 pound fin or lump crabmeat, picked through for cartilage and shell

Juice of 1 lime

Heat the oil in a pot over medium-high heat. Add the onion and cook until soft and translucent, 3–5 minutes. Add the garlic and habañero and cook until fragrant, 45–60 seconds. (Be careful not to breathe in the steam because habañeros are very hot.) Add the spinach, okra, scallion, thyme, parsley, and stock. Season with salt and pepper. Bring to a boil over high heat. Reduce the heat to medium, cover, and cook, stirring occasionally, until the greens and okra are very tender, about 30 minutes.

To finish the soup, ladle it into a blender a little at a time and purée until smooth. (I normally use an immersion blender for soups, but this soup is so fibrous, using an immersion blender was a challenge.) Return the soup to the pot and add the crab. Stir to combine. Bring to a simmer to heat through. Add the lime juice and taste and adjust for seasoning with salt and pepper. Ladle into warmed bowls and serve immediately.

Brazilian Chicken and Okra
Frango con Quiabo

Brazil is the fifth largest country in the world by population. It has many cultural influences but one of the strongest is African. According to my Brazilian friend Silvia Riedel, okra is very popular throughout the country.

MAKES 4 SERVINGS

Juice of 1 lime
3 tablespoons distilled white vinegar
2 garlic cloves, chopped
1½ pounds chicken thighs
Coarse kosher salt and freshly ground black pepper
1 tablespoon canola oil
1 onion, chopped
½ green bell pepper, seeded and chopped
2 plum tomatoes, chopped
¾ pound okra, stem ends trimmed
1 cup homemade chicken stock or reduced-fat, low-sodium
    chicken broth
1 teaspoon hot sauce, or to taste
Cooked rice, for serving

In a large bowl, combine the lime juice, vinegar, and garlic. Add the chicken and stir to combine. Season with salt and pepper. Cover and refrigerate to marinate for at least 30 minutes.

Heat the oil in a large skillet over medium-high heat until shimmering. Remove the chicken from the marinade, reserving the marinade. Add the chicken thighs to the oil, skin-side down. Cook until browned on both sides, turning once, about 5 minutes. Remove to a plate. Add the onion and green bell pepper to the skillet. Cook until soft and translucent, 3–5 minutes. Add the marinade and cook until fragrant, 45–60 seconds. Add the tomatoes and cook until softened, about 3 minutes.

Add the seared chicken and nestle the okra among the pieces. Add the stock and hot sauce. Bring to a boil over high heat. Reduce the heat, cover, and simmer until the okra is tender and juices run clear when the chicken is pierced with a fork, about 20 minutes. The chicken should register 165° on an instant-read thermometer. Taste and adjust for seasoning with salt and pepper. Serve immediately with rice.

Bahian Shrimp and Okra
Caruru da Bahia

This dish is more a stew than a side dish and is traditionally cooked until it's almost pastelike. Cashews may be substituted for the peanuts. Although the flavors are quite different from those of other dishes in this book, once again, the flavor of shrimp, okra, and rice shines.

MAKES 4–6 SERVINGS

---

1 pound large shrimp (21/25 count), peeled and deveined
Juice of 1 lime
3 tablespoons palm or canola oil
1 onion, very finely chopped
½ green bell pepper, seeded and chopped
4 garlic cloves, finely chopped
¼-inch coin of ginger, peeled and very finely chopped
1 pound okra, stem ends trimmed, very thinly sliced
¼ cup dried shrimp, finely chopped
¼ cup dry-roasted, unsalted peanuts, finely chopped
1 teaspoon crushed red pepper flakes, or to taste
3 cups water
Coarse kosher salt and freshly ground black pepper
1 bunch cilantro, leaves only, finely chopped
Hot sauce and cooked rice, for serving

Place the shrimp in a large bowl. Add the lime juice and toss to coat. Cover and refrigerate to marinate for up to 1 hour.

In a medium, heavy-bottomed skillet, heat the oil over high heat. Add the onion and green bell pepper and cook until soft and translucent, 3–5 minutes. Add the garlic and ginger and cook until fragrant, 45–60 seconds. Add the okra, dried shrimp, peanuts, red pepper flakes, and water. Cook until the okra is very tender and the mixture is thick, about 30 minutes.

Add the marinated shrimp and cook just until pink, about 3–5 minutes. Season with salt and pepper. Transfer to a warmed serving bowl and garnish with the cilantro. Serve immediately with hot sauce and rice.

Acknowledgments

Kudos to my Westchester girl who took the fast track in returning to the land of her birth and becoming a southerner via months and months of okra recipe testing.

Thanks to Mama and Jona for their neverending love and support.

Many thanks to the team at The Lisa Ekus Group for their invaluable support: Jaimee, Corinne, Sean, Samantha, and Sally, who was enlightened by the potential of spicy pickled okra as a "gateway" recipe when served bobbing in chilled vodka as a martini garnish.

Much appreciation to my dear friends and fellow cooks Gena Berry, Tamie Cook, Susan Payne Dobbs, Nathalie Dupree, Melita Easters, Damon Fowler, Elise Garner, Rebecca Lang, Matt and Ted Lee, Debi Loftis, Marvin Woods, and Charlotte Swancy of Riverview Farms.

I am very grateful for the input of a team of global okra experts: Monica Bhinde, Connie Pikulus, Sandra Gutierrez, Silvia Reidel, and Paula Wolfert.

Lastly, thanks to the University of North Carolina Press and Elaine Maisner for accepting my enthusiasm about okra.

Bibliography

Baljekar, Mridula. *Indian Cooking without the Fat: The Revolutionary New Way to Enjoy Healthy and Delicious Indian Food*. New York: Marlowe & Company, 2005.

Batmanglij, Najmieh. *Food of Life: Ancient Persian and Modern Iranian Cooking and Ceremonies*. 4th ed. Washington, DC: Mage, 2011.

Besh, John. *My New Orleans: The Cookbook*. Kansas City: Andrews McMeel, 2009.

Betty Crocker Editors and Raghavan Iyer. *Betty Crocker Indian Home Cooking*. New York: Hungry Minds, 2001.

Devi, Yamuna. *Lord Krishna's Cuisine: The Art of Indian Vegetarian Cooking*. New York: Dutton–Penguin Putnam, 1987.

Harris, Jessica B. *Tasting Brazil: Regional Recipes and Reminiscences*. New York: Macmillan, 1992.

———. *The Welcome Table: African-American Heritage Cooking*. New York: Simon & Schuster, 1995.

Iyer, Raghavan. *660 Curries*. New York: Workman, 2008.

Jacobs, Susie. *Recipes from a Greek Island*. New York: Simon & Schuster, 1992.

Jaffrey, Madhur. *A Taste of India*. Hoboken: John Wiley & Sons, 1988.

Junior League of Lafayette. *Talk About Good II: A Toast to Cajun Food*. Lafayette: Junior League of Lafayette, 1979.

Kijac, Maria Baez. *The South American Table: The Flavor and Soul of Authentic Home Cooking from Patagonia to Rio de Janeiro, with 450 Recipes*. Boston: Harvard Common Press, 2003.

Kochilas, Diane. *Food and Wine of Greece: More Than 300 Classic and Modern Dishes from the Mainland and Islands*. New York: St. Martin's, 1993.

Lee, Matt, and Ted Lee. *The Lee Bros. Southern Cookbook: Stories and Recipes for Southerners and Would-be Southerners*. New York: W. W. Norton, 2006.

Lewis, Edna, and Scott Peacock. *The Gift of Southern Cooking: Recipes and Revelations from Two Great American Cooks*. New York: Alfred T. Knopf, 2003.

Moorjani, Lachu. *Ajanta: Regional Feasts of India*. Salt Lake City: Gibbs Smith, 2005.

Nash, Jonell. *Essence Brings You Great Cooking.* New York: Amistad, 2001.

Quinn, Lucinda Scala. *Jamaican Cooking: 150 Roadside and Homestyle Recipes.* Hoboken: John Wiley & Sons, 1997.

Vaswani, Suneeta. *The Complete Book of Indian Cooking: 350 Recipes from the Regions of India.* Toronto: Robert Rose, 2007.

Yurnet-Thomas, Mirta. *A Taste of Haiti.* New York: Hippocrene, 2003.

Index